12F1
3ᵉᵛ
W9-AMT-867

A Good Place to Come From

◆◆◆◆◆◆◆◆◆◆◆◆◆

A Good Place
to Come From
♦♦♦♦♦♦♦♦♦♦♦♦
Morley Torgov

St. Martin's Press
New York

To him—in lieu of candles

A GOOD PLACE TO COME FROM. Copyright © 1974 by Morley Torgov. All rights reserved. Printed in the United States of America. No part of this book may be used or reproduced in any manner whatsoever without written permission except in the case of brief quotations embodied in critical articles or reviews. For information, address St. Martin's Press, 175 Fifth Avenue, New York, N.Y. 10010.

Library of Congress Cataloging-in-Publication Data

Torgov, Morley.
    A good place to come from.

    1. Torgov, Morley—Biography.   2. Novelists, Canadian—20th century—Biography.   3. Jews—Ontario—Sault Ste. Marie—Social life and customs.   4. Sault Ste. Marie (Ont.)—Social life and customs.
I. Title.
PR9199.3.T613Z464   1986   813'.54 [B]   86-1772
ISBN 0-312-33930-5

First published in Canada by Lester and Orpen Limited, Toronto.

First U.S. Edition

10 9 8 7 6 5 4 3 2 1

Contents

For their constant encouragement and support during the writing of this book, I am deeply indebted to my wife Anna Pearl, my children Sarah Jane and Alexander, and my friends Beverley Slopen, Lois and Jack Shayne, Lila and Alex Mogelon, Helen Mathé, Sydney M. Harris and Ben Kayfetz.

M.T.

A Good Place to Come From

It was four o'clock in the afternoon, a half hour before train time. "We better get going," my father said, snapping shut the locks on his brown valise. The businesslike tone of his voice, the sharp clicking of the locks, the firmness of his step as we walked toward the car—everything contributed to an air of determination. "It's only a two-minute drive to the station, what's the rush?" I asked. "Sure, that's right," he responded, "leave everything to the last minute, drive like a crazy fool, kill somebody, ruin a perfectly good brand new car, what do you care?" I shook my head in defeat. It was no use trying to convince him I cared.

Always, on the day my father was leaving for Toronto to buy goods for his store, there was this atmosphere of tension, this feeling of great commercial urgency: schedules to be met, judgments to be exercised (will this be a hot little item? . . . will this be a lemon?), deals to be made, money to be spent—all this to be accomplished in the garment-manufacturing jungle that was Spadina Avenue in those days. This time, however, my father was especially on edge. Earlier that day he had taken delivery of a new 1949 Pontiac sedan—his first new car since before the war. It

1

was gleaming black with white sidewall tires; parallel chrome stripes ran along the centre of the hood and continued again over the trunk lid giving the car a sleek, sporty appearance. "Look how she sits, just like the Queen Mary," my father said as he rolled the car lovingly, almost tenderly, out of the dealer's garage on Tancred Street. We made our way home along Queen Street behind the proud prominent nose of the chrome Indian head mounted atop the grille. My father's touch at the wheel was delicate, as if he were driving a crystal chandelier. Suddenly, at the corner of Queen and Bruce, mere yards away from where his own garage waited with doors thrust open to receive the distinguished new guest, rain began to fall, a soft mid-May rain. "Ach, sonofabitch!" he hissed, switching on the wipers. "Rain! My goddam luck. There must be a devil in my life. That's all there is to it . . . a devil in my life."

That had been several hours ago. Now we were on our way to the C.P.R. station at the head of Pilgrim Street. It was my maiden voyage at the helm (he had handed me the key to the ignition as if it was the key to a great city) and I drove as the historic importance of the moment dictated—avoiding pot-holes and puddles, creeping warily through intersections, while my father sat nodding with approval. He smelt strongly of after-shave lotion, having shaved—as he always did when he was leaving for Toronto—only an hour before train time. "Got to look my best," he would explain, "just in case I run into a good-looking squaw between here and Sudbury." That pre-train shave was the only festive gesture in an otherwise solemn departure routine.

I drove, and we talked . . . or rather *he* talked.

"You'll remember to double-check the cash at the end of each day to make sure it's not short or over. What's the combination to the safe?"

"Left to forty, right to twenty-two, left again to fifteen, then right again to fifty."

"Good. Try not to forget it."

"Okay. I'll write the numbers down on a piece of paper—"

"Schmeckle! Somebody'll find it—"

"So what should I do for godsake?"

"Keep repeating it. Say it over to yourself a few times every day."

"I got a great idea," I said. "Maybe I'll say it before meals, like grace."

"That's right, smart-alec, make fun. You'll see how funny it is some day when you come into the store and find the whole goddam place cleaned out . . . everything gone, stolen!"

I rattled off the magic numbers once again just to make him happy. He went on. "Remember to turn off the window lights at ten each night, don't waste electricity. You'll roll up the awning if it looks like rain but for Chrisake remember to put it down if it's sunny, it shouldn't fade the goods in the windows. And make sure you lock the garage good and tight before you go to bed. You never can tell these days who'll fool around with the car, there's so many strangers in town now. Oh yes, and stay off Wellington Street; they're putting down fresh tar on the road, the bastards, and it makes a mess of the tires."

"A person would think you're going to Europe," I said.

He sighed deeply. "Europe. I only wish to hell I was going to Europe. Anywhere but Toronto. Those whores on Spadina, I can see them now, dragging out one lousy shmateh after another, telling every lie in the book about how wonderful their crap is put together and how much they're selling to this one and to that one. Making phony promises. Gypsies, every one of 'em."

"So why do you stay in the ladies-wear business?" I asked.

"Why do I stay? Because there's a devil in my life. That's all there is to it."

As he said this, the car bounced into and out of a giant pot-hole. I grinned sheepishly. "Sorry."

"Why the hell don't you look where you're going?" he pleaded, wounded and bleeding there on the passenger side.

"I did look, honest to God—"

"If you looked, how . . . how could you possibly drive right into it?"

"I don't know. I guess there's a devil in my life, and that's all there is to it."

Staring straight ahead through the windshield, maintaining a sharp lookout for pot-holes, he sighed deeply again. "You see," he said quietly, "a university can give you an education—but it can't give you brains."

Rain began to fall again, pelting down into the face of the chrome Indian, drumming like war music against the black hood. We were almost at the intersection of Queen and Pilgrim, about to turn north to the station. "Look at this lousy town," he said moodily, "six months winter, six months rain. Sault Shtunk Marie. Same weather. Same sidewalks. Same buildings. Same faces day in, day out."

"You're just sore because it's raining on your car," I said, trying to sound cheerful. "Just think of this: if you'd stayed in Russia you wouldn't be driving a new Pontiac now, you'd be a slave to some dumb Siberian Cossack."

"What's the difference whose ass you kiss? In Russia it was a Cossack's, here it's some bitch-of-a-customer's ass. I dug a grave for myself in this town, that's all there is to it."

"So be happy," I suggested. "You're off to Toronto. A few days out of the grave."

"Every place is a grave. Russia was a grave. The Soo's a

grave. Toronto's a grave. You see this car? It's a toy, that's all. It's a toy they give you to play with, to take your mind off all the crap you had to put up with to earn the toy. It means nothing. *Jesus Christ! Be careful."*

I swung the car hard just in time to miss another giant pot-hole. "The sonsofbitches," my father said, referring to the local Works Department, "they got no respect for other people's property."

We stood on the platform waiting for the conductor's signal to board. "Every time I come here," my father said, "I think of the first time you went to Camp Borden with the Air Cadets—when was that, 1943?—and you told me on the way to the station I shouldn't kiss you goodbye in front of the other boys. When I drove away afterwards, I was so upset I wasn't sure should I laugh or cry. Now look at you. College boy. Big shit!"

I smiled and let him kiss me goodbye on the cheek.

He stood on the lowest step at the entrance to the Pullman coach, holding onto the handrail to steady himself as the train heaved and strained to overcome its own inertia. In a moment he would make the short farewell speech that he delivered always at the precise moment of the wheels' first forward motion, and that I had come to know so well.

Waving, he called out, as if pronouncing his blessing upon everyone gathered on the platform, "Goodbye Soo, fuck you."

Then he was gone.

Queen Street

Queen Street is the main street of Sault Ste. Marie. It runs east and west, roughly paralleling the St. Mary's River, for a distance of about five miles.

Today, Queen Street is lined with signs telling you it is a one-way thoroughfare heading west. You get onto Queen Street at, say, Pim, and you drive past Brock, Spring, March, Elgin, Bruce, Dennis, Tancred, Gore, travelling westward past the new International Bridge, following the setting sun all the way. Now you are as far as James Street in the heart of Little Italy. A few blocks more and you are into Steel Plant Country: Bayview, the wrong side of the tracks—smoke, dust, the grinding noises of trains and cranes, the overpowering, deep-seeping smells of sulphur and coal-tar. You obey the road signs, and you go west.

Yesterday—in the nineteen-thirties and early forties— Queen Street was a one-way thoroughfare heading east. There were no signs that told you this, only an instinct, a compelling sense of direction. You got onto Queen Street at, say, Huron, and you passed about two dozen streets as you travelled eastward, stopping—if you were a Gentile—at Simpson Street where the stately red brick houses and the

6

green lawns were; not stopping—if you were a Jew—until you had gone as far east as you could go: east along Highway 17 and eventually along Highway 11, passing through Sudbury and North Bay and Huntsville, until the road signs said "City of Toronto" some 500 miles later. Then, and only then, did you stop.

For the smalltown Jew, and especially for the children of the smalltown Jew, Queen Street was a one-way street heading eastward to Toronto. There could be no stops in between.

The people of whom I write—the thirty to forty families who made up the local Jewish community—occupied stores and apartments and houses within a relatively small area in the central part of Sault Ste. Marie. The intersection of Queen and Bruce Streets formed the hub of this area, and most of the Jewish business establishments and homes lay no more than a block or two from that point. Despite this apparent concentration, it is impossible to characterize the inhabitants as ghetto-dwellers, nor was this a shtetl environment in the European sense of the term. As you walked along Queen Street, you saw, true enough, signs that read "Himmel's Ladies' Wear," "Friedman's Department Store," "Fishman's Men's Wear." You heard two neighbouring merchants call to each other on the sidewalk, "Hello, Joe," "Hello, Isaac." You heard Mr. Cohen and Mr. Mintz greeting each other in Yiddish outside the Royal Bank. Yet you were not conscious of being in the midst of a Jewish world. It was as if the Jews—even those who owned their own properties—were no more than temporary tenants who borrowed time and space on Queen Street during daylight hours in order to make their living. To the Gentile population, we were a mysterious subterranean breed, a race who surfaced daily from 8:00 A.M. to 6:00 P.M. (midnight on Saturdays) to sell merchandise, and disappeared into the ground after hours to do God-knew-what. There were no Jewish theatres, delicatessens, butcher shops, corner confectionaries; none of the storefront street-level institutions one associates with the ghettto. Until the mid-1940's there was no synagogue.

If there was little resemblance to the big-city ghetto, there was even less resemblance to the shtetl. Having been blown across Europe by a hundred different winds of turmoil, and having vomited their way across seas and oceans to North America, our fathers were far too worldly to live the life of simple villagers. They had shaved off beards and sidelocks, discarded skullcaps, eaten pork when it meant the difference between living or starving, battled with the English language and called down plagues upon its unfamiliar spellings and pronunciations. They worked on the Sabbath, indeed worked harder and longer on the Sabbath than on any other day of the week, for that was the one day of the week when the Gentiles were most often in a spending mood. To nothing—save the inescapable curse of old age—did they resign themselves. Before no one did they bend or cower. The rabbi was always no more than a few minutes away, ready to be consulted when the spirit was low or the conscience was tortured. But somehow he could never be the symbol of rigid, orthodox discipline that his shtetl counterpart had been in Europe; rather, he could only be one of them. Granted he hadn't shed the trappings of his religion as they had done; nevertheless, the same gales that had carried them like pollen from one continent to another, had carried him as well. He and they were comrades, shipmates, fellow-tenants.

Not ghetto Jews, not shtetl Jews. What then were they? Upside-down weeds . . . that perhaps is the best way to describe them. Weeds that had planted themselves in strange ground, weeds that grew with their foliage—the fruit of their labours—submerged in the earth and their roots exposed to air and sky. They spent their lives this way, scratching, scraping, building up, tearing down, conniving and surviving. Always there was the struggle to invert themselves, to establish root and leaf in proper order, to become more than mere weeds, to become indigenous plants.

They never entirely succeeded.

My father demobilized himself from the Russian army late one night in the summer of 1917. Reluctantly he had spent two years and eight months in the service of the Czar and his lack of enthusiasm for military life only deepened when the Czar was eliminated and the Bolsheviks moved into the royal palaces. The southern part of Russia, near Odessa, where my father had been born and raised, was famous for producing great watermelons and violinists, both of which products my father loved, but these attractions were not powerful enough to draw him back to a land which was also famous for producing misery and cruelty. Taking liberty without leave, he headed in the direction of Roumania and never saw Russia again. Nine years later, his tour of the Western World came to an end in a small, northern Ontario town, the name of which he could barely pronounce —Sault Ste. Marie.

In the interval between his self-demobilization and his descent at the Soo's railway station, he had dabbled profitably in the currency market in Roumania, earned the price of a steerage ticket to "Kanada," harvested wheat in Saskatchewan, taught Hebrew in Winnipeg where he married the older sister of one of his pupils— a prize catch because she had been born in England and her father was a man of property who had once been reeve of West Kildonan. After Winnipeg, it was peddling made-to-measure suits to miners in Timmins, doing business out of the back of a horse-drawn wagon. For engaging in this enterprise without a transient licence, he was arrested and fined $50.00. That experience crystallized his thinking. It was high time to stop being a transient.

But where to settle?

In the financial circles frequented at the time by my father (i.e., the roving bands of fellow peddlers and other here-to-day-gone-tomorrow types), word was spreading about the golden promise of a town with a crazy French name which they pronounced "Sahlt-stee-maria." The Algoma Steel plant there was taking on hundreds of immigrants from Italy and the Slavic countries. The town held potential riches for a clothing man who didn't mind working eight days a week, could communicate in the foreigners' lingo, and was fast with a tape measure.

Sault Ste. Marie society little noted nor long remembered the day my father and mother, anchored by a large steamer trunk, disembarked at the railway station at the head of the street appropriately named "Pilgrim Street." To the by-standers on the station platform who eyed them with only casual interest, this was simply another greenhorn and his wife come to town to hustle yard goods and ribbons. But to the handful of Jews already there, the new couple would be welcome company. Would this mean a fresh source of competition? Yes. Sometimes, however, in this semi-wilderness, it was better to lose a dollar here and there and gain a landsman, a neighbour from your part of the old country, someone who spoke Yiddish, could perhaps quote a bit of Talmud, someone who slurped tea from a glass through a sugarcube held between the front teeth, and remembered what the watermelons were like in the south of Russia.

Before long, the town began to yield some of its golden promise: a small shop on Queen Street, a self-contained flat over the shop, a Model T, and for the first time, a feeling of permanence. The young Russian Jew, still sporting the pencil-slim moustache he had affected years before in the Russian Army, and the quiet Winnipeg girl who worked at his side day and night in the shop despite the fact that she was now very pregnant, were here to stay.

Like most of his fellow merchants, my father was everything in the business—merchandise-buyer, window-trimmer, window-washer, cashier, stock-controller, salesman, even seamstress on occasion. And like most of his colleagues in the trade, he depended heavily upon his wife who assisted him in nearly all of these diverse functions. But there was one ritual in which he relied entirely upon her. That was when the "Inspector-Generals" made the rounds. The Inspector-Generals were women who customarily travelled in pairs, visiting one store after another along Queen Street. They would finger their way through long racks of dresses and try on every hat in the place, whispering furtively to each other in Italian or Ukrainian or Finnish, never committing themselves one way or the other, but examining each garment critically at arm's length. Truly an outsider at such moments, the merchant could do nothing but stand idly by, wondering whether the Inspector-Generals were planning a purchase or plotting a pogrom. At last, one of the women would speak up: "Where Missus?" That was the signal for the merchant's wife to come forth. If "Missus" neither spoke nor understood these foreign languages, she was at least fluent in the international language of hemlines and bodices; therefore, "Missus" usually clinched the sale, turning the tricky, final stage of the transaction—the price haggling—back to her less gentle husband.

When it came to male trade, it was a different story. Here the merchant himself took over exclusively because this aspect of the business involved a fine art known as "sidewalking." My father would position himself on the sidewalk directly in front of his emporium, standing well out towards the curb so that he had a commanding view of the eastern and western approaches. His competitors up and down the street stationed themselves similarly on the sidewalk in front of their establishments. All of them pretended not to notice each other. Then, from a distance, the merchants could spot the first contingent of spenders. They might be steel workers just finished the night shift, still grimy and sweaty, carrying their empty lunchpails and bearing those most important fortnightly pay cheques in their wallets. Or they might be lumberjacks just arrived in town on the Algoma Central from the "bush", desperately needing hot baths and fresh clothes, their pockets bulging with a winter's pay. Whether or not the steel worker or lumberjack had a familiar face was immaterial. As soon as the fellow was within hooking range, my father would call out to him, "Hey, Mike! [It was always assumed that the man's name was Mike] . . . Mike, come on in. I got some real good buys for you today. Gotta nice suit for you for Easter. C'mon, Mike!" The next thing Mike knew, he was standing before a full-length mirror draped in the latest blue serge or black pinstripe. The fitting of such a garment involved a degree of ingenuity and virtuosity never dreamed of in Saville Row.

These smalltown Jewish merchants had learned the art of fitting in the "tuck-and-pull" school where a suit was literally yanked, stretched, jammed and cajoled into shape in an exercise that amounted to an outright assault upon the customer's sagging body. The physical effort was accompanied by grunts, sign language, quips in the customer's native tongue, Yiddish oaths. Finally, sighs of relief from both vendor and purchaser as the last pin was pressed into place in the trouser cuffs. When the ordeal was over, the merchant would stand back to admire his handiwork. "Mike," he would assure the fellow in the mirror, "you'll be the talk of Queen Street on Easter Sunday, believe me." Before Mike had time to agree or disagree, he was choosing a shirt, matching tie, socks, shoes. The split-second Mike was out the door, having left behind him a fair chunk of his pay, the shopkeeper was back once again at his sidewalk stand, calling out to the next available steel worker or lumberjack, "Hey Mike, c'mere . . ."

The social life of the Jewish community revolved around a suite of two rooms rented in the second storey of a building near the corner of Queen and Bruce. Located within easy reach of nearly all the Jewish stores and homes, the shul had the advantage of convenience. But that was all.

The smaller of the two rooms was occupied as a cheder for the children as well as a place for memorial services. Here the young were instructed and the dead remembered, all in an atmosphere of mustiness and overcrowding. The room constantly reeked of cigarette smoke and ancient mildewy prayer books. Even when the windows were opened wide, fresh air refused to venture within; instead it hung outside in the bright sun, beckoning children to come out and play. The men, swaying idly to and fro as the rabbi murmured and chanted, stared longingly out of the windows and daydreamed of sitting in rowboats, fishing and munching hardboiled eggs.

The larger of the two rooms was much too large for the average community function. Therefore, it was used very little, mostly for special occasions—High Holiday services, Bar Mitzvahs, weddings, benefits. Long wooden benches ran along the walls of this chamber, leaving a vast empty space in the middle. Thus it was quite impossible to make an entrance or exit without the entire congregation's eyes falling upon you and without attracting comment. "Look at that, he just got here and already he's running back to the store" . . . "Look at Queen Esther, if you please, sneaking in a minute before the service is over so God should think she was here all day" . . . On Yom Kippur, late entries and hasty exits were dead giveaways: "Aha, the bastard's just come from breakfast" . . . "There she goes, couldn't wait like the rest of us until the rabbi blows the shofar" . . . It was a seating arrangement designed for conspicuous prayer only; private sacrilege was quite out of the question.

The worst feature of the larger room was that it lacked exclusivity, since it was also the local headquarters for the Independent Order of Foresters. Indeed, the Foresters had the main claim to the premises and filled the walls with their regalia. There were photographs of officials all posing stiffly and sternly as if guaranteeing posterity that the Foresters would always be independent and stand for order. Huge framed charters, adorned with red wax seals and gold ribbons, proclaimed the legitimacy of the local branch. Shields were mounted in recognition of noble collective efforts, and plaques honoured all sorts of individual acts of self-sacrifice.

Only a dull cabinet that cried for a coat of varnish belonged to us. It stood against the east wall of the room and housed the two Torahs during High Holiday services and Passover. All the rest was Foresters' property, in Foresters' territory.

The two rooms were connected by a dimly-lit corridor where the boys gathered to exchange dirty jokes and tease the girls, and where everyone gathered occasionally as a diversion from religious devotions, to listen to a Finnish husband and wife who occupied an apartment on the same floor, screaming at each other in their native cacophony.

In 1946, after years of fund-raising, planning, debating (put ten Jews together and you immediately had ten architects), the first synagogue was consecrated. At last the congregation possessed its own building, a modest red brick structure on a modest plot of land on—where else?—Bruce Street, not far from its intersection with Queen.

I wonder: in all the years preceding the opening of the new synagogue, how many little Jewish kids were convinced, as I was, that God was actually a member of the Sault Ste. Marie Lodge of the Independent Order of Foresters?

Why did we, the children of the smalltown Jews, leave home? Why this perpetual motion eastward?

There are a thousand and one reasons, but they all boil down to a single reason: we left because our parents counselled us to leave, begged and pleaded with us to leave, even ordered us to leave. Only yonder in the big city, they insisted, could one be a truly big person; here in this town, one could be no more than a large fish in a tiny pond. Better to be the tail of a lion in a great city, than the head of a jackal in Sault Ste. Marie.

We, the children, resisted at first. Life seemed so simple,

so attractive in the small town.

There was little, if any, overt discrimination against the pocket-size Jewish community. Happily for us, the Gentile population was too engrossed in a civil war of its own to pay us much attention. It was a cold war, waged between the Anglo-Saxons of the East End and the Italians of the West End. The latter group, who numbered many thousands, were beginning to look eastward from the Latin Quarter towards Simpson Street. Dr. Mancini, recently graduated, preferred to live in the same fashionable part of town as old Dr. Macmillan. Old Dr. Macmillan was prepared to tolerate Dr. Mancini at meetings of the local medical society, but having Dr. Mancini and all the little Mancinis residing next door to the Macmillans was another matter. So totally did this conflict occupy the two principal racial establishments that somehow we Jews were able to slip out from between the two sides and maintain a state of neutrality. Besides, a handful of Jews such as we could scarcely pose any threat even if we *had* become partisans in the struggle. So we kept our feelings to ourselves, smiled compatibly at both major factions, and simply carried on selling them noncombat merchandise—clothing, furniture, scrap metal—in return for which they were gracious enough to pay their bills and leave us in peace.

And what of the eternal quest to earn a decent livelihood —wasn't it easier in the small town? Our fathers had planted the saplings for us, had endured the Depression, had prospered through the war years; now all that remained for us to do was to nourish the orchards and harvest the fruits. Every afternoon there was lunch at home and a short nap. In the summer, you could close your store at six and be sitting down to supper at your cottage at Pointe-aux-Pins by six-thirty. Wednesday afternoons there was fishing at

Garden River or Echo Bay, a few miles down Highway 17. Who needed fancy college degrees? Who needed the urban rat race? Who needed suburbia?

On the surface, it was an effortless, uncomplicated existence.

But our fathers and mothers knew otherwise. Beneath the paper-thin crust of their serenity, volcanoes were boiling. Gone were the days of "sidewalking;" now there were petty jealousies and, sometimes, bitter competition as business rivals strove to consolidate the gains of the war years and expand their tidy fortunes. Fathers and mothers stewed privately and publicly about the love affairs of their sons and daughters: how could young David ever find and settle down with a Jewish girl if, instead of venturing forth to Detroit or Toronto, he stayed put on Queen Street and took out schiksas on Saturday nights? What could be done to prevent young Miriam from becoming too involved with that shaygetz from Pim Hill, the fellow with the Irish surname who kept taking her to Hi-Y dances and Boat Club regattas? The same people saw each other all the time. They did the same things all the time. The men played cards around the dining-room table, while the women sat in a circle in the living room and gave each other recipes (often deliberately omitting a key ingredient or a crucial measurement, a favourite bit of one-upmanship). Old-timers who knew each other intimately, too intimately in fact, were getting on each other's nerves. The neighbourly pat on the back was beginning to leave claw marks.

How ironic it is that the years from 1939 to 1945—in many ways the best years of their lives—had left these small-town Jews stale and worn out, fiercely determined on the one hand to hang onto the narrow but secure patches of life they had cultivated for themselves, but equally determined that their children should cultivate far different patches in far-away metropolises.

Thus, my father, surveying all he had accumulated, did not turn to me and proclaim, "Some day all this will be yours." Rather, he looked about him at the racks of suits and dresses that were in style today and out of style tomorrow; at the Inspector-Generals who still managed to make their rounds despite their arthritis and fallen arches; at the bleak, black silence of Queen Street on a February night when it seemed that the only thing stirring in the whole world was a solitary snow plough. And all he said was, "Get out, get out before it's too late".

And I did. I got out before it was too late.

Semper Paratus,
Semper Fidelis,
Semper Annie

We thought she was dying. She stood at the door of our apartment that Saturday morning pale and shivering. With both hands she gripped a badly worn suitcase that had been tied round with twine for reinforcement.

"Don't tell me you walked on a morning like this!" my mother said. It was February, the harshest time of the year in Sault Ste. Marie. All life was deep in the annual winter standstill, caked in ice, buried in snow. "Come in, come in for heaven's sake." My mother waved the girl in. "You can put your suitcase down in the hall for now. Sit down and warm up for a few minutes," she said, gesturing toward the kitchen.

Slowly, carefully, as if fearing to damage the cheap wooden kitchen chair that was offered, the girl sat down. Her hat and coat and gloves were still on. She rubbed her gloved hands together, uttering low hissing sounds as the cold burned its way out of her fingers and the numbness departed telling her she was still alive.

I took a chair at the kitchen table where I sat appraising our new maid. She looked at me, but her face hadn't thawed sufficiently to permit any form of recognition that I was there. After a long minute of silence, I asked, "Do you know the words to 'Red Sails in the Sunset?' "

She nodded no.

"Do you know the words to 'The Isle of Capri?' "

Again she nodded negatively.

"I learned some new words," I said. I began to sing, "Twas on a pile of debris that I met her . . ."

The girl began to laugh. She laughed self-consciously, without parting her lips, stifling herself so that she would not appear too forward in the strange household.

I followed the girl as she went to the closet and withdrew a hanger. She placed her coat on the hanger, hooked the hanger over the closet bar and closed the closet door—doing all these acts with the same slow, careful motion with which she had sat on the kitchen chair. It was as if everything in the apartment was sacred and fragile.

"Are you Italian?" I asked.

"No," she answered quietly.

"Our last girl was Italian. She taught me some funny words in Italian. Do you know how to say 'Kiss my behind' in Italian?"

The girl flushed—the first sign of colour in her face—but before she could answer, my mother intervened. "Don't listen to him," she said to the girl. "He's got an awfully big mouth for a nine-year old."

I was determined to track down the girl's racial origin. "Are you Ukrainian? We had a Ukrainian girl once. And before her we had a Croatian girl and before her—"

"I'm Ukrainian," the girl said, interrupting my short history of family domestics.

"Can you teach me some Ukrainian? The last Ukrainian girl that worked here taught me how to say—"

"Never mind," my mother cut in again. To the girl she

said, "Come, I'll show you to your room and you can unpack. You'll stay in our son's room." My mother talked as she led the way, like a tour guide. The girl followed her, walking with timid steps lest she should disturb the precious linoleum underfoot.

I sat on the edge of my bed watching her unpack. Why she needed twine to secure the suitcase I don't know; there were very few items within.

"How come you've only got that much?" I pointed to the small pile of clothing she had arranged on what was to be her bed. "The last girl, the Italian one, she needed two whole drawers in my dresser to put her stuff into."

"I guess she was pretty fancy," the new maid replied.

"She wasn't so fancy. I heard my mother and father talking after she left. My mother said she left some underwear in the dresser and was it ever dirty."

The girl turned and smiled at me. "You've got awfully big ears too." She had small teeth, white and even, and when she smiled, her wide face with its high cheek bones seemed to become even wider, giving her a pleasant countenance. I decided I was going to like her.

"Is your name Annie?"

"Yes. How did you know?"

"I took a guess," I said, proud of my acumen. "Most of the maids I've seen in people's houses are called 'Annie.' "

She made no comment on this observation. A small boy's generalizations, right or wrong, flattering or insulting, had to be accepted when one was just starting a new job with the small boy's parents. She continued laying away her clothes in one of the drawers.

"We're Jewish," I said. "We eat a lot of things that Ukrainians eat, like stuffed cabbage for instance."

"I know. Except you people put meat in yours. We just

put rice in ours. I know some girls who work in Jewish homes and they've told me. They say Jewish people eat a lot of meat. Every day, too."

"Is that why you're coming to work here?"

She made no response.

I guessed what part of town she came from. "You're from Bayview, I bet." She nodded; I was right again. "They all are," I said.

I knew Bayview well. It was in the extreme west end of town, the section that lay in the soot and shadows of the steel plant. The streets there were unpaved, and in the summer, dust rose from the roadways to meet the yellowish smoke descending from a multitude of plant smokestacks nearby, the two combining to smother people and animals and houses in a dense, ugly pall. In winter there was no dust on the roads; instead there was slush hardened into tortuous ruts that defied pedestrian feet and automobile tires. In all seasons the yellowish smoke and the smell of sulphur lingered heavily in the air.

I had gone often to Bayview, travelling there twice a month with my father while he made the rounds collecting— or attempting to collect—bills that had been owing by his customers for weeks, months, even years. I would wait for him in the car, playing behind the steering wheel and making furious speeding noises, while he entered one unpainted house after another, his accounts books in hand. In warmer weather his customers would come out to the car to greet him, extravagantly complimenting him on his clever, handsome boy, occasionally offering cookies or fresh produce from their backyard gardens, but almost never tendering cash. It was always the same frustrating pattern on those visits to Bayview: a few words exchanged between merchant and customer in some Slavic tongue or in broken English, a pat on the back, and goodbye, see you next month. On the return drive to the centre of town my father would always mutter, "Didn't collect five cents and now I've got to wash the goddam car again."

That was Bayview. That was where they were from, these girls in their late teens or early twenties who worked for the Jews "downtown." Their own families were hopelessly over-populated and underfinanced in these Depression years. As soon as each girl was old enough to scrub an acre of floor and wash dishes for ten people—a state of the art usually reached early, say, at fifteen or sixteen—she immediately became available for domestic service. Through a mysterious grapevine that transmitted "Help Wanted" cries all the way from Queen Street East westerly to Goulais Avenue in Bayview, news of such a girl's availability quickly spread. If the girl's older sister had preceded her into the market, the faults or the virtues of the elder—telegraphed along the same grapevine—usually influenced the speed with which the younger found employment.

The salary—ten or twelve dollars a week—could hardly be called liberal, bearing in mind that the girl's typical day, repeated six times weekly, began at seven in the morning with the preparation of breakfast and ended at nine in the evening when the last dish had been dried and the youngsters in the family had been coaxed into bed.

But there were compensations. The girl, accustomed to sharing a room at home with perhaps four or five sisters and brothers, was now reduced to a single roommate or, if she were lucky, she might even have a room all to herself. And then there were three meals a day, one of which always featured meat or fowl. Often there was a large family-size bottle of orange or cola-flavoured "Kik" on the table, a beverage that had originated as a Sunday-lunch luxury but eventually became as indispensable as a mezuzeh in the average Jewish home.

This was the life to which our new maid could look forward.

Except on Sundays, we ate all our meals in the kitchen. The maid always ate with us. My mother and father seldom lingered over breakfast or lunch. Both worked in the family clothing store downstairs and had little time for second cups of coffee and idle chit-chat. Even in these dreary doldrum days, they seemed possessed by a sense of commercial urgency. There might be whole days when barely a customer came into the store, yet they had to be there. There were "things to do," always "things to do."

It was the same on this February Saturday afternoon. Lunch had been eaten quickly, then my parents were off downstairs again, my father calling to my mother, "Come, there's things to do . . ."

We were alone—the girl and I—at the table.

"Do you like being a maid?" I asked.

"I don't know. I guess it's alright." Her voice was flat and she played with her fork, jabbing it into the mound of untouched cottage cheese and sour cream on her plate.

"Did you go to school before you came here?"

"Yes. I was in grade ten at Tech, but I had to quit."

"You going to get married?"

"No." She thought for a moment, then added, "Maybe someday, I guess. I'm going with a boyfriend."

"What's his name?"

Reticently the girl looked down at her plate, prodding her cottage cheese with her fork into a compact mound. "Pete. Peter Lisanti. My folks say they'll kill me if I ever marry him. He's Italian, that's why." I nodded wisely, pretending to understand.

The following day—Sunday—the girl had been given the afternoon off to spend at home with her family. My father drove her to her house in Bayview. On his return he stamped his feet and clapped his hands trying to generate warmth in his limbs.

"I went inside their house for a minute," he told my mother. "My God, how can people live like that?"

He described the cardboard patches on the walls, the wood-burning stove that served as the central heating system, the dilapidated furniture, the bread crumbs and finger smudges.

"And kids everywhere," he exclaimed. "Wherever you look there's a kid. I just don't know how people can live like that. We shouldn't be paying these girls, they should be paying us. We're actually doing them a favour when we take them in."

"You have to feel sorry for people like them. Look at it that way," my mother said. "Besides, I couldn't be in the store six days a week without a girl in the house, you know that."

My father said nothing; he knew she was right. But his thoughts were still back in that house, that broken-down frame cell situated at the dead end of a bleak street in Bayview. He had seen these houses many times over the years, but he would never grow used to the sight.

"Pheh!" was all he could say. Shaking his head sadly, he repeated it quietly to himself, over and over again, "Pheh!"

That evening, after Annie had returned, she came into my room—which was now "our room"—carrying a paper shopping bag. I was already tucked away for the night but had stayed awake waiting for her. Whispering so my parents wouldn't know I was still up, I called to her.

"Annie?"

"You still awake? Shame on you. Don't you know it's almost ten o'clock?"

"What's in the bag?"

"The rest of my clothes."

The room was dark except for a sliver of light coming through the door that had been left slightly ajar. "You can turn on the light if you want to," I said.

"It's okay. I can see what I'm doing." She withdrew her belongings from the shopping bag and pressed them into the drawer. "There," she said, sounding satisfied, "that's everything."

"Why didn't you bring all that in the first place? There was enough room in your suitcase, wasn't there? Did you think maybe you wouldn't be staying?" I asked.

"Goodnight nosey," she whispered back. "Go to sleep."

I heard her in the dark undressing and putting on her pyjamas. A couple of minutes later I called to her again. "Aren't you going to brush your teeth?" She didn't reply. She was sound asleep.

On the following morning, the official training program began.

Even before she had sat down for her first meal at our table, Annie had been instructed very emphatically to remember at all times that there were two sets of dishes on the shelves, one "meat," one "milk;" she was never to mix or confuse the two. Already aware of this peculiarity from gossiping with other "Annies," the girl nevertheless politely pretended to be impressed with what my mother termed "Lesson Number One." This lesson also offered a two-minute course in Hebrew dietary laws—again unnecessary since word of our bizarre food conventions and eating ceremonies had been circulated throughout Bayview by other girls who had ventured eastward into Jewish dwellings. Still my mother felt bound to remind Annie of the various prohibitions that surrounded the shelves, stove, icebox, and anything in the place that had to do with victuals. Annie responded on this Monday morning by burning the porridge and letting the coffee boil over. My mother fretted; my father said it was nothing, the kid was nervous, that was all.

In the ensuing weeks, as she had done with the girl's predecessors, my mother played Professor Higgins to Annie's Eliza Doolittle.

"Annie, don't say 'youse,' it's you, just you . . . what would *you* like for lunch, not what would *youse* like" . . . "Annie, be sure you tie a kerchief around your head when you're preparing food; last night my husband found a hair in his borscht" . . . "Annie, when you make a bed, always be sure to tuck the bottom sheet well in, like this" . . . "Annie, when people call on the phone, always say 'Hold the line, please,' not just 'Wait a minute'. . ."

Like Eliza, Annie learned well. In fact, so uncommonly well did she learn that my mother was toying with the idea of adopting several little housekeeping touches which, hitherto, only the wife of the wealthiest Jew in town had dared institute.

"I was thinking," my mother said one night, eyeing my father cautiously, "I was thinking maybe we should have Annie wear a uniform. Nothing fancy, just a plain black dress with a white collar and apron. Instead of a house dress. It would be so much nicer when we have company."

My father was silent, hidden behind his Jewish newspaper.

"And I thought maybe we should get a little bell for the dining-room table. It's nicer than calling her, or having to run into the kitchen to get her when it's time to serve another course."

My father's reaction, predictably, was immediate, clear, and final: "No!"

At that point—just short of uniform and summoning bell —the reshaping of Annie-Eliza stopped. But if Annie's growth as a maidservant had achieved its maximum, her relationship with me was still reaching for its highest level. Indeed, our relationship blossomed daily. She taught me more Ukrainian words, opening up to me narrow but very entertaining horizons of Slavic obscenity. She hadn't known the lyrics of "Red Sails in the Sunset" that first day. No matter. Pete Lisanti, who called for her every Saturday night, took her to all the musical movies at the Algoma Theatre and she and I together learned just about every song that came out of those wonderful, dreamy, fantastic films of the day—songs crooned by Dick Powell, Fred Astaire, Eddie Cantor, Bing Crosby. On the third day of Passover, when I could no longer bear the sight and sound of unleavened bread, she smuggled an O Henry bar into my room and there, while she stood guard at my door, I huddled in the dark, devouring my favourite confection, eternally grateful to my Ukrainian benefactor, and not giving the slightest thought to harder times when my people were slaves under Pharaoh.

She became my confidant, I became hers.

My confidences were, of course, entirely juvenile. They concerned teachers whom I planned to assassinate, quarrels with other kids and suitable revenges, lost nickels and dimes, newly-won friendships with girls at school, and a myriad of petty likes and dislikes.

Her confidences were far less childish. Of her affection for Pete Lisanti she spoke often; how she admired his dark complexion and his shiny wavy black hair, how marvellous he looked in his hockey outfit when he played right-wing for the James Street Aces, how much he yearned to get out of the steel plant in a year or two and try out for the Detroit Red Wings. She was sure he would make it. Then they would marry and move to Detroit and she would accompany him on the road and journey to cities like Boston and New York and Montreal. They would never have to live in a place like Bayview. And her parents, seeing what a famous athlete and loving husband Pete was, would put aside their hostility and accept their Italian son-in-law with open hearts and arms.

We respected each other's confidences. When cross-examined nightly by my father about how long I had practised the piano, I would lie and say a whole half-hour, which was the prescribed period, when in fact I had shaved the time down to twenty minutes. Annie could always be counted upon to bear witness for me. "Oh yes, I checked the clock and he definitely practised for half an hour like you told him." For my part, I never so much as dropped a hint to my parents about Annie's and Pete's intentions for fear they would report these to Annie's parents, thus triggering a wholesale race riot in the West End.

Often we talked in the darkness of my room, long after I had been put to bed and she had dragged herself into her bed exhausted from the day's labours. Sometimes, instead of talking, we hummed the latest hit tunes from the movies, doing so quietly to avoid detection by my father and mother. I had developed a deep affection for Annie, as well as a fierce loyalty. After all, were we not in a sense co-conspirators?

One night, as we lay discussing the state of our respective worlds, Annie confided something new to me.

"Promise you won't say anything to your folks?"

"I promise. Cross my heart."

"Well, you know what I can't figure out? I can't figure out why they won't eat anything but kosher meat at home because it's against your religion, but when they go out to a restaurant they eat meat that isn't kosher and they have bread and butter with it and things like that. Why is that?"

I thought about it for a moment. "Gee, I don't know. Maybe it doesn't count if you eat it in a restaurant. Whenever we go to the Chinaman's place across the street, my Dad lets me have bacon. Bacon comes from a pig but he lets me have it anyway. In fact, sometimes he has bacon, too."

"Do you like bacon?"

"I'm crazy about it!" I said.

Annie said no more on the subject that night. The following Saturday night, after supper, my parents announced that after the store closed—which would be about ten o'clock when the last potential customer on Queen Street had finally wandered home—instead of coming directly up to bed, they would be going to a house party and wouldn't be back until about midnight. As soon as they had disappeared downstairs, Annie went to the icebox. "Look!" she said, holding up a small cellophane-wrapped package she had extricated from under a pile of larger parcels at the bottom of the icebox.

"Bacon!" I cried excitedly. "For me?"

She fried it the way I liked it, crisp and crinkly, so that it tasted delicious even when it had cooled. Together we consumed the whole package. Then we scrubbed the frying pan and cutlery and even the dishes with cleanser, and checked and double-checked the stove and kitchen counters to make certain that every possible tell-tale sign of God's unchosen meat had been eliminated. To that extent the exercise in deceit was a success. There remained, however, one problem: even a person with one nostril would be able to tell in a second that bacon had been cooked here. The smell of hot bacon grease clung to the apartment and everything in it. It clung stubbornly, tenaciously. We opened doors and windows. We burned brown sugar in a saucepan. We waved towels and even blankets in the air, hoping that this crude form of agitation would rid the apartment of the odour. All to no avail. By midnight enough of the smell of bacon still resided in the apartment to indicate to any normal person with two nostrils that evil deeds had been committed involving pork in some form or other. There was nothing to do but go to bed and pray that the Angel of Forgiveness would descend and fill the place with some magical scent, before my parents arrived home.

Unfortunately, the Angel of Forgiveness was on holiday that weekend. The next morning, Annie was obliged to undergo a stern refresher course in Lesson Number One. As for me, there was very little hope.

"This is how it all begins," my father shouted. "First you eat bacon in your own house; the next thing you know you're bringing pork chops to the table, the next thing after that it's saying grace and going to church. You might as well marry a schiksa now and get it over with!"

Considering that I was at that time still in public school, the thought of marriage to anyone, let alone a Gentile girl, had never crossed my mind. What did marriage have to do with crisp crinkly bacon? Why was it permissible to eat "traifs" across the street at the Chinaman's but not here, in my own kitchen? What had Annie done that was so dreadful?

"I don't understand," I said that night to Annie in the privacy of my bedroom.

"Neither do I," she admitted. "But never mind. One of these Sundays I'll take you home with me on my afternoon off. Maybe my mother'll make bacon for supper, and you can have some with us."

Many Sundays came and went after that, and I waited patiently for the important invitation to accompany Annie home to Bayview. At last, one Saturday night as she waited for Pete Lisanti to call for her, she said to me, "Tomorrow, if you like, we can go to my house for the afternoon."

"Can I have some bacon?" I asked.

"All you want," she promised.

My father hadn't exaggerated. Annie's home in Bayview consisted of a paintless, frame house slouching on a narrow wasteland of cinders. A few weeds grew there by mistake; otherwise, everything was dying, oblivious to the fact that it was late spring. Inside the small house, every corner declared the family's near-bankruptcy.

Annie's father—a stocky, unkempt man who carried half the steel plant under his long, black fingernails—greeted us with a heartiness that belied his poor surroundings. He bent down, laughing in my face, saying, "So this is the little Jew who likes pork, eh!" A strong odour of beer gusted into my nostrils. I knew at once the source of his good cheer.

Standing behind the head of the house, Annie's brothers and sisters—all younger than she—stared at me as if I were little Lord Fauntleroy, making me feel both unique and slightly uncomfortable.

The woman of the house—Annie's mother—was an older version of Annie: same full face and wide cheekbones, same thick legs and wide hips. She wore a hairnet and a sleeveless, cotton housedress cut with wide openings around the neck and shoulders, more for ventilation, I assumed, than for style. Her skin resembled boiled chicken. Apart from a perfunctory grunt in my direction, she ignored me completely and busied herself at the wood stove cooking something in a large soup pot.

The father motioned to a chair in the centre of the

kitchen. "Sit down, sit down, little boy," he urged. He poured himself a glass of beer. "Beer!" he said, holding up the glass and grinning.

"None for me, thank you," I said.

"Oh no, not for you, beer not for little boy." He laughed very hard. "Beer for me. No give beer to little boy. Police come. Big trouble, eh."

He downed the beer in one gulp, and began to pour himself another glass.

As he did so, his wife swung round from the stove and spat something at him in Ukrainian. In a flash his expression changed to wild-eyed rage and he slammed the glass down upon the kitchen table, spilling beer across the printed oilcloth. Vehemently he flung some expression in Ukrainian back at the woman. Suddenly she, too, was transformed. What I took to be a taciturn and rather feckless old woman in an instant had become a human blast furnace, spewing foreign words all over the kitchen like molten slag. For emphasis she kept banging a heavy ladle against the soup pot on the stove, while her husband resorted for his special oratorical effects to slamming that remarkably durable beer glass down upon the kitchen table again and again. Bang went the ladle, clink went the beer glass. Bang–clink–bang–clink-bang-clink—in a riotous duet not unlike Verdi's "Anvil Chorus." I couldn't understand a word the two said, but the tempo and the volume of the argument were clearly augmenting. I began to resign myself to the fact that my long journey here by streetcar and on foot would probably prove to be in vain when suddenly Annie's mother pointed her soup ladle at me and let go another barrage of words in her high-pitched voice.

I turned to Annie. "What does she want?"

"She wants you to sit down. Supper's ready."

With the exception of Annie's mother, we all sat down. The father, calm again, even a little genial, presided over the table. Like a king he helped himself to the food placed in bowls before him: boiled potatoes, steamed cabbage (*un-stuffed*), some green onions and radishes. With an iron-worker's grip he clasped a horseshoe-shaped garlic sausage to his chest, carving off small chunks and letting them fall into his plate the way one slices a banana. Then he pushed the bowls of food toward his wife. She saw to it that everyone's plate was filled before she took the leftovers for her own plate and sat down at her place. We ate in silence broken only by the smacking of lips and the clatter of dishes and cutlery. I kept looking over at Annie, not daring to say with my voice, but trying desperately to say with my eyes, "Haven't they forgotten something?" But they hadn't forgotten, for presently Annie's mother withdrew from the oven of the wood stove a pan of bacon which had been fried earlier and placed there to keep warm.

"Here boy," the father said, pressing a stack of bacon strips on his fork and dumping them helter-skelter in my plate. "Eat, eat."

I wolfed down the first few pieces with enormous zest. The thin strips of meat had become dry in the oven and the rind was as tough as a leather bootlace. Still, it was bacon, and I gorged myself, not paying the least attention to the fact that I was the only one at the table eating it. Annie's brothers and sisters sat observing my private feast, their expressions— as before—impassive. Annie's youngest sister leaned over to Annie and whispered something in her ear, to which Annie responded with an annoyed "Sh!"

Annie's father's geniality continued to expand as I ate. "Good bacon, eh? You like?"

"It's my very favourite," I mumbled, talking with my

mouth full. Then, after a moment, I added, "Well, almost my very favourite. I love spaghetti just as much. Annie's boyfriend is going to take me to an Italian restaurant soon for spaghetti and meat balls."

My host scowled. "What boyfriend?"

"Pete Lisanti," I responded airily, popping another piece of bacon into my mouth.

The scowl deepened, the voice took on a dark tone.

"How you know Pete Lisanti?"

"He comes to our house a lot. I like Pete. He says some day when Annie and him are married—"

"My daughter no gonna marry no bloody dago," the father cut in quietly, looking sternly over at Annie. Annie looked at me and seemed about to say something, then she turned away and stared at the floor beneath her chair. Her father rose without taking his eyes from the girl. Then, as before, there came a violent outburst. "My daughter no gonna marry no bloody dago!" This time he shouted the edict at the top of his lungs. Annie's mother too got up from the table and began shrieking at Annie in Ukrainian. I watched the drama from my corner of the table, completely fascinated by what I was seeing and hearing, not in the least conscious of the betrayal I had inadvertently committed.

Annie, the poor wretched victim, could stand the tirade no longer. She ran from the table in tears and disappeared into one of the bedrooms adjoining the kitchen, slamming the door behind her. Now everyone was deserting the table—the kids to run outside and escape the tumult, the father to pace up and down the kitchen, the mother to sit in a corner of the room rocking and swaying her body and moaning to herself, "Oi oi oi oi . . ."

I was alone, little Lord Fauntleroy in my Sunday best, quietly demolishing the remnants of a pound of bacon, wetting my fingers and catching up tiny bacon crumbs on my plate and on the oilcloth, while around me the people of the house—like the house itself—were dividing and crumbling.

Not until the horn of my father's car sounded outside the house at dusk did Annie emerge. Her eyes were red-rimmed, her mouth drooped sorrowfully. The horn sounded again. "Come on," was all she said to me. She said goodbye to no one in her family, and no one said goodbye to her. I started to follow her out to the car, then turned to say thank you to Annie's mother and father but they were gone.

"Well, did you have a good feed?" my father asked, shifting the car into gear.

"It was fine," I answered. Through the car window I could see Annie's brothers and sisters still staring at me in their dispirited way. A lone light on the street had just lit up. In the air floated the familiar smell of sulphur. Behind us, as we drove off down the roadway, the dust billowed up and Annie's house disappeared.

Annie remained with us for almost a year after that Sunday. Then she left, as we knew she would, to marry Pete Lisanti. In the interval between that visit to her home and her departure from ours, she never again confided anything in me beyond her feelings about the weather or her intentions to manicure her nails. But I continued to trust my little secrets to her and never once was my trust misplaced or violated. Pete never did take me for spaghetti to an Italian restaurant and my passion for bacon was confined to the Ritz Café across the street, a not-so-ritzy establishment run by an exhausted-looking Cantonese who was said to have lost a fortune in the stock market.

The wedding—to which we were invited—was a terribly stiff affair, held in a Roman Catholic church. Annie's parents, staunch Greek Orthodox, sat unsmiling on one side of the aisle; Pete's sat unsmiling on the other. Annie and Pete borrowed a car and honeymooned for a week in a rented cabin near Batchawana Bay, north of the Sault. Before long they had three kids of their own and a small frame house in the West End near the heart of "Little Italy." Pete switched from the James Street Aces to the Marconi Flyers. Then he injured his back at the plant and had to give up hockey.

Annie and Pete never left the West End.

Room and Keyboard

The boy in the *New Yorker* advertisement is about nine or ten. Well-scrubbed and neatly attired, he's the kind of kid you see on a Saturday at F.A.O. Schwarz's being presented with an expensive birthday toy by an adoring grandmother from Scarsdale. He stands with one hand boyishly tucked in his trousers pocket, the other resting casually on a piano bench, all poise and self-assurance, a typical young Manhattanite who divides his time between penthouse and private academy. The copy beneath the picture glows with high hope: "He'll be playing a Steinway, the piano played by most professional pianists, which should add some incentive to his practice hours." The writer of this bit of prose may know a great deal about pianos and piano virtuosi. What he knows about boys, on the other hand, doesn't amount to a hemidemisemiquaver.

I stare at the advertisement and suddenly I am the boy in the picture. It is October, 1935. Voices are speaking to me, at me, over me, and around me.

"What do you mean you don't want to learn to play the piano?"

"Everybody nowadays plays piano—"

38

"Show me one house in this town that doesn't have a piano?"

The voices, rising in pitch and intensity with each delivery, are those of my mother and father. It is Saturday, lunchtime. The table bears leftovers from last night's traditional Friday night supper, reheated except for the remainder of a chicken which we eat cold with H.P. Sauce. A traditional Saturday lunch. It will soon be time for my parents to return downstairs to the store to make the final push for the week. ("If you don't make a dollar on Saturdays, you might as well close up altogether.") More important to me, the Saturday matinee at the Algoma Theatre begins in less than an hour. Burgess, my redheaded freckled friend will soon be knocking at the door. There will be a dime for the movie, a nickel for a chocolate bar, and a couple of hours of re-enacting with Burgess that day's episode of the Tarzan serial after the show is over and we are let out blinking in the late afternoon sun. Why can't they just let me eat my cold chicken and H.P. Sauce and leave me in peace?

This is the fourth or fifth meal in a row during which I've been forced to sit through these persuasions. I look anxiously at the kitchen clock. One thirty. A half-hour to go before the lights go out in the Algoma and that marvellously menacing M.G.M. lion flashes onto the screen, its impatient roar drowned out by cheering and whistling and stamping feet. The voices continue, pressing, reasoning, unreasoning.

"Remember *Top Hat*? The minute you came out of the movie you knew every song by heart, some even with the words! Fred Astaire didn't even sing them so good. I'm telling you you got a brilliant ear. It's a shame not to use it."

"And it'll be fun. Your father'll play his violin and you'll play the piano and the two of you can perform at parties sometimes."

Compared to glorious freedom in the streets of Sault Ste. Marie, the idea of musical togetherness at home is hardly a temptation. Even less tempting is the prospect of a father-and-son act. I see my father looking benignly down at me over the bow of his instrument, and I see myself in a velvet suit (like Freddy Bartholomew but even less appealing because I wear eyeglasses) playing dainty little trills and being hugged by bosomy old women and cheek-pinched by their paunchy old husbands. I'm the darling of the Sunday afternoon tea-and-spongecake set. What will my boyfriends say? It is almost too horrible to think of. Indeed, so overcome am I by the horror of it that tears form, collect around the lower rims of my glasses, and roll down my cheeks dropping one by one into my soup. My mother prudently slides the soupbowl out of range. "It's salty enough already," she says.

Now they are reminding me that Irving Cohen, who lives a couple of blocks away, is only a year or two older than I and already he is in Grade Eight of the Toronto Conservatory piano course. The comparison infuriates me. Why must I always be compared to kids who are totally abnormal, kids who will engage willingly in the most unnatural activities just to ingratiate themselves with their elders? Irving Cohen, whom I have by turns scorned or ignored in our chance meetings, is now Private Enemy Number One on my list. Angrily I cry out, "I don't care what Irving Cohen does! I hate Irving Cohen!"

Finally comes that last-resort word—please. "Please," my father urges, "just take one lesson and see how you like it."

"But we haven't even got a piano," I argue back, hopelessly, my voice choking into a pitiful squeak.

"We'll get one. I'll look in the paper. Somebody always has a piano for sale."

Burgess stands in the doorway slapping his tweed cap

against his thigh. It is late and he is impatient. I rush past him, my glasses tear-stained, and he turns, bewildered, to run after me. In my hand I clutch a dime for the movie, a nickel for the chocolate bar, and an extra dime—ten whole cents!—to spend as I please.

I have given up, caved in, knuckled under. I will be a piano player.

It is one week later. I have come home from school to find a piano standing in the hallway outside our apartment, like some strange timid monster waiting to be invited inside to become part of the family. Once the struggle to squeeze the piano through the front door is over, my parents stand back, appraising their latest acquisition.

"I think we got a bargain at thirty-five dollars," my father says.

"Yes, but don't forget you had to pay the movers on top of that," my mother says, a strong hint of disapproval in her tone.

My father defends himself. "I couldn't help it. The old lady said she needed thirty-five dollars clear to bail her son out of jail." But my mother is unconvinced. "I still think you could've made a deal for twenty-five. We're not million-aires, you know."

Not millionaires indeed. Still, in these arid penny-pinch-ing times, when it is often difficult to find a chicken in every Jewish pot, how customary it has become to find a piano in every Jewish living-room! Our home will follow this pound-foolish custom, except that the huge ugly-brown in-strument—after being denied lodging in the living-room (too cramped), in my parents' bedroom (too private), in the kitchen (too cluttered) —finally ends up in my bedroom at the rear of the apartment.

That room—windowless, sharing a frosted-glass skylight with the adjoining kitchen—exists in a state of half-darkness even on the brightest days. It is an area that begs for more sun and a bit of breeze. Instead it now receives within its four walls this gloomy monolith, keys yellowed and chipped, innards thickly coated with dust, and a middle A that probably hasn't vibrated four hundred and forty times per second since the day it was first struck at the factory.

"Where did the old lady keep it?" my mother asks, screwing up her nose. "The whole piano smells like bacon grease."

"I'll fix that soon enough," my father assures her, and promptly dumps a bag of mothballs through the top of the piano. I can hear them cascading through the strings and springs and hammers.

My mother screws up her nose again. "Now it smells like bacon grease and mothballs," she says.

What can this hideous piece of furniture possibly add to my life that I should be forced to cohabit with it? I think about the old lady's son and how lucky he'd been in jail. Imagine, a cell without a piano.

My father hisses obscenities in six Eastern European languages as he scrapes and rubs and polishes the instrument. The piano-tuner (who swears in English only) seizes one tool, hurls down another, mutters angry orders to himself, pounds middle A with his right index finger until both finger and note are exhausted. Finally, the strings have been tamed and the tuner puts down his pliers, seats himself at the keyboard, clears his throat, and plays at full volume one chorus of "I Love Coffee, I Love Tea." My mother laughs with amusement, and my father urges the tuner to play another chorus. I stay well in the background, praying that this toolbag Paderewski will fracture his fingers.

Now there is a man seated next to me on the piano bench. His hands, bony and bluish (he has walked over a mile in the raw November night to give me my first lesson) rest on the keys and he explains in a cultured English accent that I must pretend I am holding an orange in each of my hands. I can smell Sen-Sen on his breath as he examines my outstreched fingers the way a gourmet examines fresh beef to see if it's properly marbled. "We'll have to get rid of that webbing between your fingers," he says, looking solemn, like a surgeon about to cut. "At the moment your hands look like duck's feet."

"The Cohens told us that their Irving had the same trouble with his hands at first," my father says.

"Lots and lots of good solid practice, that's what does the trick," the teacher says. Father and teacher nod solemnly. The rapport between them, established only minutes ago, is now centuries old.

"Irving Cohen does a half-hour in the morning before school, fifteen minutes at lunch, and a whole hour at night. And on Saturdays and Sundays he sometimes plays two hours straight without a stop." As he recites these statistics my father looks grimly at me, I look grimly at the teacher who in turn looks grimly at my father. We are, the three of us, a new phenomenon in the world of music—The Grim Trio. I am miserable, but presently misery gives way to hatred. I hate Irving Cohen even more now. And I realize that he and I are now destined to become rivals. My father is already burnishing the family armour. "Don't worry," he tells the piano teacher, "just give this kid of mine a year and he'll be up to Irving Cohen. The whole town'll be talking about him."

It is two years later. We are in the Foresters Hall, a large, draughty room which ordinarily serves the Jewish community as a place of worship, but which tonight has been transformed into a theatre with a low, hastily-constructed stage, a curtain consisting of several white bedsheets, and some blue and white paper streamers draped in a limp and unimaginative fashion from the light fixtures on the ceiling. The final curtain has been drawn on the annual Purim play, the last curtain calls have been taken by the child stars, and the proud parents in the audience are busily trading compliments. There follows a short, musical concert. One untalented child after another steps sheepishly to centre-stage. Some sing songs, two young violinists scrape together a duet, the melody of which begins uncertainly and disappears entirely by the third or fourth bar. A trumpet player threatens to blast down the walls of Jericho for a second time in history. Everyone is off-key.

Now the master-of-ceremonies stands at centre-stage, beaming back at the roomful of beaming parents. "The time has come to hear from Ahasuerus and Haman," he announces. This introduction greatly amuses the audience, and the master-of-ceremonies is very pleased with his little joke. I, too, feel satisfaction for in my role as King Ahasuerus I have had the pleasure on this night of condemning the evil villain, Haman—played by Irving Cohen—to hang. The sight of Irving being dragged off to the gallows has provided me with spiritual uplift, and I recall praying that he would stumble from the stage and crash-land right on his web-free fingers.

Haman, having suffered a humiliating death in the play, is invited to play the piano first, a courtesy which I welcome in the belief that he who plays last, plays best. Irving is seated at the piano. He is too shy to turn and face his audience, and merely mumbles over his shoulder the title of the piece he will play. No one quite catches the title, and I manage only to catch the words "by Johann Sebastian Bach." (I learn later by peeking at his music book that it is a prelude and fugue.) His fingers are swift and accurate. And the voices in the fugue mesh with the precision of well-tooled gears, the whole piece building strongly to a stirring, concluding major chord. There is a moment of silence. Rising from the piano bench, Irving turns and bows stiffly. The audience is cold; this has been cerebral music, music that is not of the heart. The applause, therefore, is merely polite and dies quickly. Irving moves awkwardly across the stage before the silent crowd and returns to his seat.

"His teacher's that German fellow," someone whispers.

"Goddam Germans. They're all alike. Everything comes out like from a machine," another responds.

"And now King Ahasuerus, please," the master-of-ceremonies calls, milking the situation for one more laugh.

I begin to play the opening phrases of Johann Strauss' "Tales of the Vienna Woods," and as I pass into the main theme, an "ah!" of recognition rises from the crowd. I have chosen wisely and I play the piece reasonably well, schmaltzing up my performance by playing the waltz rhythm of the left hand "rubato" in the shameless style of a band of gypsy restaurant musicians. Rustling leaves and chirping birds flow from my right hand. We are so deeply immersed in the Viennese woods that one or two people in the room are moved to hum or whistle along with me. I cannot spot my father and mother among the patrons, but vanity tells me they must be exploding with pleasure. The last grand chords bring down the house.

But I do not stop to accept the accolade; instead I rush off the stage and out of the room, making straight for the privacy of a nearby lavatory. There I fling "Tales of the Vienna Woods" into a waste basket.

Later, at home, my father is triumphant. "Didn't I tell you someday he'd be ahead of Irving Cohen? Didn't I say the whole town would be talking about him?'"

"Stop saying those rotten things about Irving," I shout. "He's better than the whole bunch of you put together!"

My father and mother exchange bewildered glances.

"All of a sudden Irving Cohen is your hero?" my father asks.

I make no reply. My father and mother will never understand what has happened to me on this night. They will never understand that I have come face to face with my own cheapness, and the cheap tastes of the well-meaning audience. In shoddiness, we have been joined together, the audience and I, and I am ashamed of the union.

I exhibit my contempt for Johann Strauss, and for his devotees, and for myself, by deliberately playing "The Blue Danube Waltz" with my left hand in the key of C and my right hand in C-sharp. The dissonance is wall-crumbling.

My father is furious. "You're ruining a good piano," he cries.

"Then stop making me play this lousy Jewish music," I yell back. ("Jewish" music, according to my father, is any kind of music that has heart and soul, and into this broad category he has lumped Tchaikowsky, Chopin, Schumann, Rubinstein and practically anybody else who has written an easily hummable tune or a melody in a minor key.)

"I suppose that German anti-semite knows what's good music, eh?" my father says derisively.

In the end I win. At my next lesson, my piano teacher shows up with two new volumes which he places ceremoniously before me at the piano—Bach's two-part inventions, and a book of Mozart's sonatas.

The days of toy music are over.

On the following Saturday, Burgess is at the door.

"I won't be going to the Algoma today," I say to him. "I'm going to Irving Cohen's house. Maybe I'll see you after the show gets out."

Burgess is off like a shot, a happy redhead bound for an afternoon with Hopalong Cassidy and Buck Rogers.

I am bound for an afternoon salon with Irving Cohen, and two composers whom I have never heard of—Debussy and George Gershwin. I have become a twelve-year-old snob.

It is 1943 and Irving Cohen and I are now two of the leading lights in the local musical world—a world that consists largely of Tony Dionisi's Dance Band ("the band that makes dyin' easy"), the Canadian Legion Fife and Drum Corps, an assortment of teachers and musicians who frequent Anderson's Music Store to play records on Saturdays, and another assortment of teen-age zoot-suited music lovers who feed the nickelodeon at Capy's Grill on Saturday nights. It is a world very much alone in space; there are no other musical planets nearby, no stars out there in the bleak universe. The town has yet to be visited by a string quartet, let alone a symphony orchestra. Solo artists—those few who dare to perform for the folks who live at the end of the railway line—are usually second-rate, on their way up to, or well on their way down from, virtuosity. The local radio station carries the Metropolitan Opera broadcasts on Saturday afternoons and the New York Philharmonic concerts on Sundays; apart from those two programs most of the air time is taken up with country-and-western and, of course, the big bands of the time—Miller, Shaw, Dorsey.

Irving is the painstaking technician, given to spending a whole afternoon at the keyboard working on a single passage until each bit of fingering has become second-nature to him. Though he remains shy and awkward in front of an audience, his technique is awesome. Under his fingers, Chopin's "Black-Keys Etude" emerges from the pianoforte like bullets from a machinegun—rapid, precise, forceful. I, on the other hand, rely on charm, plus massive applications of the loud pedal, to see me through the trickier spots. I have a kind of romantic bedside manner that lulls audiences into overlooking careless octave runs and blurred trills.

I have also become a war hero. I am one of the performers at a public concert to boost the sale of war bonds, and am in the midst of pounding out a passionate rendition of Sibelius' "Romance" when a gooseneck lamp perched atop the vibrating upright piano begins to edge forward. The lamp is irreversibly bound to a collision course with the keyboard, but I nevertheless continue playing. Precisely at the sound of the next loud base-note, the lamp plunges down coming to rest just a few inches above the keys where it dangles by its cord, like Damocles' sword. The audience gasps but, without missing so much as a grace note, I carry right on (those war bonds must be sold!), finishing the Romance with a dramatic flourish. Following which I rise and calmly restore the lamp to the top of the piano. The next day I am hailed in the local press as "a courageous young artist." Like Aladdin and Florence Nightingale, I have established my reputation with the aid of a lamp.

"Play us a little tune" has become a standing inside joke with Irving and me. No matter where we are, if there is a piano in the room, someone will pipe up with "Play us a little tune" and we are expected to be gracious and without further urging seat ourselves at the keyboard. There is no end to this shotgun concertizing. Furriers from Toronto, pants manufacturers from Winnipeg, dress salesmen from Montreal—it makes no difference. Each and every one is assumed to be a devotee of "good music." Singly or in groups they are corralled into the living-room ("I don't care how busy you are, you must hear my son play the piano . . . ") where they are obliged to sit through all three movements of a Mozart or Beethoven sonata before they can write so much as a dollar's worth of business. To a commercial traveller, whose only genuine aim is to sell his merchandise and get the hell out of Sault Ste. Marie on the next train, this mandatory musical interlude must be sheer agony. Irving and I compose special numbers for these occasions: "Prelude To The Sale of a Pair of Pants," "Overture to Overalls," "Fanfare for Furriers." There is more than a tinge of malice in this, for we are shrewd enough to sense the traveller's agony and perceptive enough to realize that he doesn't care a hoot about Mozart or Beethoven.

Given such a thin cultural atmosphere, what sustains us and helps us to flourish? It is something we have developed which I call "The Gershwin Game." Thanks to Irving's initial discovery, Irving and I have become Gershwin addicts, totally caught up in the music, the lifestyle, the wit, the lore and the legend flowing from and created around that composer. For hours at a time we play recordings of the *Rhapsody in Blue,* the *Second Rhapsody, Cuban Overture, American in Paris,* the *Three Piano Preludes,* the orchestral suite from *Porgy and Bess,* the popular show songs, and above all, the *Concerto in F.* We read and re-read aloud passages from Oscar Levant's book, *A Smattering of Ignorance,* until we have memorized whole pages of dialogue between Gershwin and his friend-confidant-exponent-

and-biographer. Irving takes to wearing a bar-pin through his shirt collar in the style of Gershwin and I buy my first double-breasted suit to give myself that snappy New York-in-the-thirties look. Since Sault Ste. Marie has no Broadway, we imagine that the lights that line the canals and locks on the Michigan side of the St. Mary's River are the bright lights of the theatre district. A booth at the back of Capy's Grill becomes our Algonquin Round Table, occupied exclusively by two pseudo-sophisticates. From the other booths the uninitiated view this make-believe with a mixture of curiosity and suspicion. When the waitress brings Irving's chocolate sundae and mine, Irving points to his—which has extra whipped cream—and, borrowing a Gershwin line, says, "You see, that's the difference between genius and talent." At the end of an evening during which Irving has monopolized the keyboard at my house, I borrow a Levant line, "An evening with Irving Cohen is an Irving Cohen evening." It goes on and on and our parents and friends begin to wonder when it will end.

It ends in June, 1944. "Gershwin," who is now of draft age, joins the United States Navy. "Levant," who is not yet old enough for military service, stays behind in Sault Ste. Marie. The passion for Gershwin's music goes on. But The Gershwin Game is over. One person alone cannot play.

Twenty years have gone by. Irving Cohen has helped to win World War II off the coast of China, has finished a fine arts course at a university in Michigan, and has married. His family has left Sault Ste. Marie and I have lost track of his whereabouts and career. I am married, have two small children, and reside in the middle of a carefully planned network of cul-de-sacs and dead-end streets in a suburb of

Toronto. One day the telephone rings: "Hello, it's Irving
. . . Irving Cohen . . . I happen to be passing through
Toronto . . ." We meet and for a few minutes The Gershwin Game is on again, revived with great enthusiasm and
laughter.

At last the conversation turns to the present.

"What're you doing with yourself these days?" Irving asks.

"I'm a lawyer. What's your line?"

"Hospital linens. Sheets, pillow cases, towels. Best line in
the trade. Competition can't touch our stuff for quality.
We've got this new line on the market now—real soft
finish, launders like a dream. A lot easier on the patients,
you know; cuts down on bedsores and nuisances like that.
How about you, are you specializing in anything?"

"Business law. You know—real estate, mortgages, cor-
porate deals of various sorts. Do you still play a little piano
once in a while?"

"No, not much," Irving replies. "I've changed my whole
lifestyle over the years." From his jacket he withdraws a
slim leather case and offers me a cigar. "Jamaican. I like
'em better than Cuban. Go ahead, take one, they're great."

Full-cheeked and thick-lipped, like two contented bull-
frogs, we sit blowing thick clouds of cigar smoke into the
air. "Did you read recently that George Gershwin suffered
from chronic constipation all during his adult life, and that
he visited brothels from time to time?" I ask.

"You're kidding?" Irving responds, smiling incredulously.

"Honest-to-God."

"Too bad about Levant," he says, snapping his gold cigar
clipper open and shut. "He sure turned into a wreck. I saw
him try to play part of the slow movement of Gershwin's
Concerto in F one night on Jack Paar's show. What a
disaster!"

"I guess you and I were smart to stay out of the music business."

We nod in agreement. Two men who made the right decisions years ago, each at his own point somewhere along the path that leads from genius to talent, and from talent to reality.

The Guest Speaker

What did we know about anything?

Highly educated we weren't. Well informed we weren't. Neither were we makers of news; indeed we didn't even live anywhere close to makers of news.

There were no supper-hour pundits on the radio interpreting events for us while we ate our beef-and-barley soup, no celebrity-commentators appearing on a television screen nightly at bedtime to issue grave warnings or forecast promising upturns for tomorrow. The news, like the moon, had its dark side—a side none of us could see or comprehend. Only local gossip could be discussed in depth and with authority; after all, first-hand rumours were always more reliable than second-hand knowledge.

So when you got right down to it, what did we really know about anything?

Not much. But we did possess a deep thirst. We yearned to see and to hear someone in our midst—anyone—who could stand up and say, "I know . . . I was there . . . I saw with my own eyes . . ." We were like parched prairie earth that waits open-pored for the rains.

At last the rains came.

The gods—that is, the executive of one of the Jewish charitable agencies in Toronto—had heard our prayers and sent us an elderly scholar, a man in his late sixties or early seventies, to enlighten and inspire us in the backwoods.

He was to speak to us about the Jewish Homeland in Palestine. The occasion therefore called for a full congregational meeting: men, women, children, even babes in arms. Wooden folding-chairs crashed, the smells of coffee and smoked fish drifted over the room from the refreshment table set up at the back, parents confiscated yo-yos, admonishing their kids at the same time to pay attention and learn something.

The guest speaker, accompanied by the chairman, made his way through the noisy audience to the head table and sank heavily into the only armchair in the place. Perspiration shone from his broad forehead. He was flushed and obviously having difficulty catching his breath.

"The steps must have been too much for the old man," someone whispered. (Two long flights of steps had to be climbed to reach our third-storey meeting hall.)

"Naw," someone replied, "he just ate supper at the rabbi's, that's all."

The latter diagnosis was correct. The speaker had indeed supped at the rabbi's, stuffing himself—or being stuffed by his generous hosts—with the sort of meal that provided ballast against strong winds and rough currents: boiling hot soup, fish, a variety of meats and poultry, the traditional leaden puddings, all laced with enough garlic and spices to power a city for a year.

The chairman began: "Tonight it is my great pleasure and privilege . . ." As he fumbled painfully over his own syntax and polysyllables, I studied the old man who sat at his side basking sweatily in the glowing introduction. He was short and dangerously fat, filling his blue serge suit so fully it resembled a fresh tube of toothpaste about to disgorge its contents. His collar and tie fought against each other to maintain their respective rights around his ample neck. The buttons of his vest struggled to be free of their holes and threatened at any moment to explode from his chest, fly like fragments of shrapnel across the meeting hall, and embed themselves in the ceiling and walls.

Fifteen minutes had now gone by and the chairman mumbled and stumbled on. Having outlined the history of the guest's birth in Russia, his education (a yeshiva in Odessa, seminars with this famous rabbi, discourses with that learned professor), the chairman reached the point of the young scholar's departure by ship for America.

The same voice that had earlier diagnosed the guest's respiratory troubles spoke again in a loud whisper.

"I'll bet it'll be a slow boat. Look who's the captain."

He was right. The "captain" was making the most of his hour at the helm. During the next ten minutes, that liner touched every port in the Mediterranean, spent two endless days and nights lying over for supplies at Gibraltar (here we were treated to a cave by cave description of the famous rock), heaved and tossed its way across a stormy Atlantic, and steamed—at long last—into New York Harbor ("past that magnificent lady with her arm upheld beckoning the poor and the tired . . .").

The poor and the tired. I looked at the uncomfortable corpulence seated in the armchair. All these years had passed, I thought, and he still looks poor and tired. Still, there was an intellectual air about the man, no denying it. The clothes, slightly shabby and poorly fitted in the first place, bespoke a man whose cares centred around library and book, rather than closet and wardrobe. The thick bifocals, the right index finger pressed against his temple, the assortment of fountain pens arrayed like medals across the pockets of his vest—all these signs pointed to a profound man, a man who thought only important thoughts, a man to whom even a routine weather report must have carried deep philosophical overtones.

The chairman had now transported us to a soul-stirring day in the mid-thirties when the scholar was about to set foot on Palestine's soil for the first time. "Imagine, ladies and gentlemen, the thoughts which, in these times of trial and tribulation for our people, moved the mind and the heart of our esteemed guest as he gazed upon those shores where once Moses . . ."

Another loud whisper behind me: "The sonofabitch always has to grab the limelight—"

"Shah!"

"Shah my ass. I came here to listen to the speaker from Toronto, not the chairman from the Sault."

Heads turned, eyes glowered, the chairman came to a full stop, freezing the action in Haifa Harbor just as the guest of honour was halfway down the gangplank. Boldly the backseat critic rose to his feet.

"Are you gonna let him talk or aren't you?" he shot at the chairman.

"When you're the chairman you'll run it your way. Right now I'm the chairman and I'm running it *my* way."

Chairman and critic glared at each other, then critic sat down. But it was too late now. The chairman couldn't find his place among the dozen sheets of foolscap spread before him on the lectern. His timing, never exactly masterful, was now completely destroyed. Like Captain Queeg's, his self-confidence had been shattered; his ship was floundering—it was time to get off the bridge. Left stranded on the gangplank, the speaker would have to disembark in his own words.

"I suppose," the chairman said icily, glaring still at his unruly opponent in the audience, "I had better let you hear the rest of the story from our distinguished visitor himself."

The abruptness with which he sat down took everyone by surprise, most of all the guest of honour who didn't appear ready to rise, now or ever. An awkward silence fell over the room. The chairman turned to the guest, gestured toward the lectern, inviting the old man to take the floor.

The speaker gripped the arms of his chair and, with a mighty effort, made it to his feet. Once on his feet, he seemed about to fall forward across the head table and would indeed have done so, had the chairman not pushed the lectern in front of him in the nick of time. Leaning wearily on the lectern, he stared at the sheaf of notes before him. Everyone waited. At last he looked up and spoke.

"Water . . . I need a little water, please . . ."

A pause while a jug of water was produced. One glass, two glasses, and part of a third were consumed before the speaker uttered another word.

He began sotto voce, partly I suspect because it was his style to begin very quietly and build to a climax, but more because the repast upon which he had gorged himself several hours earlier was only now beginning to inch its way down his esophagus and into the vast tunnel that formed his digestive tract. That words emerged from his mouth at all under these circumstances was miraculous.

"I speak to you this evening at a difficult time."

This opening statement, pronounced with profound gravity, drew a slight titter from some members of the audience.

"I feel a great weight upon my heart, and pain in the very depths of my soul [widespread titters, plus one outright chuckle that quickly turned itself into a polite cough] as I stand before you to relate what is happening."

At this point the speaker halted. He was attempting to suppress a belch, and obviously succeeded, although where the wayward pocket of air found a vacancy inside that well-packed interior, heaven only knew. Wherever it was, it was immediately joined by the remainder of a third glass of water, then a fourth. Momentarily relieved, the speaker looked out over the audience once again, earning a round of applause mixed with laughter. There being no gavel, the chairman slapped a book down hard upon the table.

"Please, let us have some order and respect." He gestured politely to the speaker to continue. Instead, the speaker bent laboriously toward the chairman. A whispered conference between the two, and anxious glances toward the doors leading from the hall, told what was next on the agenda. Taking the old man solicitously by the arm, the chairman led him from the head table toward one of the doors. The moment the door closed behind the two, the audience—men, women, and children (those old enough to understand)— broke into uncontrolled laughter. The rabbi, whose generosity as a host was exceeded only by his love of a good joke, abandoned the dignity of his station and laughed until his cheeks were crimson behind his white beard.

It may be said that the elderly scholar emerged from the same door wherein he went. In fact he was obliged to do so no fewer than four times during the course of his speech. Each time he excused himself with great feeling: "Please, please you must pardon me . . . I'm so sorry, so very sorry . . ." But on each successive return the applause grew until it was almost an ovation. Had he been capable of sustaining such a performance, he would no doubt have attracted standing-room-only audiences within a few nights for by now he had become the object of sympathy as well as amusement, the perfect comic hero.

Considering that his lungs and arteries, not to mention his other vital body mechanisms, had functioned overtime throughout the evening, his final declaration rang out with astonishing vigour: "Praise be to God the Jews have turned the desert into a blooming garden!"

Too exhausted to acknowledge the enthusiastic hand-clapping that greeted the end of his oration, and too weak even to accept another glass of water that was offered, the old man slumped into his chair.

"I'm sure I speak for the whole Jewish community," the chairman said when the applause had ended, "when I say how truly inspired we are by our guest speaker's glorious and important message."

More enthusiastic applause.

"And I am confident," he went on, "that each of you will now want to look into your heart and respond to this great man's emotional challenge that we should contribute to the welfare of our less fortunate brethren in Palestine."

The chairman paused and peered sternly over his spectacles in the direction of the cluster of men in the assembly. No handclapping now. Just absolute silence.

"You didn't tell us there would be fund-raising," one of the men called out.

"Come, come now," the chairman called back, "you didn't come here just to eat herring and onions, did you?"

Amid general mutterings of discontent, there commenced a tribal ceremony known as "on-the-spot collection." The ritual (which the congregants would undergo on many occasions afterward) proceeded thus:

Stage One: A tense stillness in the air. Everyone waits for one or other of the two "rich ones" to open. Meanwhile the two "rich ones" eye each other cagily, neither daring to make the first move. This is the orthodox Western gunfight, but in reverse—the object is to see which gunfighter has the *slowest* draw. Having hung back as long as honour will permit, one of the two finally announces his commitment. The other quickly matches it.

Stage Two: Murmured criticism on the part of the bystanders because the rich ones opened scandalously low or— even worse—uncomfortably high.

Stage Three: The momentum builds slowly downward as, one by one, the men in the audience call out their pledges and begin writing out their cheques.

Stage Four: An awkward minute or two as "the poor one" makes up his mind.

Stage Five (Final Stage): A collective sigh of relief.

The ordeal of giving was over. Without awaiting further formalities, the audience rose from their seats and fell into noisy chatter. One knot of disgruntled donors immediately huddled in a corner of the room remote from the head table, to plot the ruination of the chairman. The chief plotter— a strict authoritarian at home but an unfettered anarchist away from home—occupied the centre of this group, inflaming his small band of cohorts with angry talk. "If I told you once, I told you a million times, you cannot trust a Galitzianer. May they burn in a fire, every one of them!" In another corner were gathered "The Four Hundred," those few in the congregation who considered themselves more affluent and sophisticated than the general run—the cream of the cream, the chosen of the chosen. At their centre, holding court, stood the wealthiest entrepreneur, delivering a travelogue; he hadn't been to Palestine, but he had been to Florida recently and in the eyes of his courtiers he enjoyed at least as much celebrity status as the guest speaker. Close by the refreshment table, the town glutton and gluttoness, an obese couple who lived from snack to snack, carefully stationed themselves within easy reach of a large platter of spicy baked carp, thus gaining a two-seconds advantage over their nearest rivals, a poor second-hand furniture dealer and his wife for whom two slices of carp were often a full-course meal. Liberated from parental control at last, the children erupted all over the room releasing two long hours of bottled-up energy.

With the arrival of the first steaming samovar, the chairman, the plotters, The Four Hundred, the uncommitted, and the kids all joined in the crush at the refreshment table. In their resolve to get at the platters of food they were —as always—unanimous.

In the front rank, pressed against the refreshment table, stood the guest speaker, filling his plate—a human silo storing food to sustain him over the hundreds of miles of railway track that stretched from the Sault to the next Jewish outpost on his itinerary.

After him, there came other guest speakers from time to time. Mostly they were younger men. Some were poor scholars, thin, attired in loose-fitting black suits, their pale faces bearded; verbal stuntmen who spoke almost entirely in Yiddish and quoted from memory Hebrew sayings out of the Old Testament and Talmud, none of which they took the trouble to translate but all of which sounded erudite and impressive. Their voices rose and fell dramatically, and they performed little ballet movements with their shoulders and arms as they pleaded in this wilderness for faith and charity. When they ate, they pecked at their food furtively, like crows.

Others were portly businessmen from Toronto who stepped off the train in expensive overcoats with velvet-

trimmed collars. They spoke in English and drew their
quotations from Shakespeare ("If you prick us, do we not
bleed?"), but most of the time—being men of affairs—they
relied upon facts and figures, graphs and charts, to make
their points. Invariably they were on diets and ate with
extreme caution, politely rejecting second helpings, swallow-
ing little white pills discreetly with their tea, joking self-
centredly about their ulcers and the strains of operating
large clothing factories and travelling on speaking circuits
during the off-season.

All of them—though their talents varied—threw their
hearts into their tasks. But not one of them came close to
matching the old man's effectiveness. It was one thing to
speak from the heart. And quite another to speak from the
heartburn.

Being Prepared

The Great Debate of '38 began on the eve of my debut as a full-fledged Boy Scout. Tomorrow—Sunday—our troop would march from its home base, Central United Church, along Albert Street to St. John's Anglican Cathedral for a joint service with other local troops. The route was a mere city-block in length, but for me the occasion—my first parade—held all the significance of Caesar's return to Rome from Gaul. I stood before a full-length mirror fussing with my brand-new uniform, adjusting and re-adjusting the Mountie-style hat, centring and recentring the red and grey neckerchief, pulling the navy-blue hose so taut they wouldn't dare wrinkle. In response to my own orders—shouted at the top of my voice—I practised snapping to attention, standing at ease, and saluting.

All this drilling my father tolerated in silence, hidden behind his newspaper. But I could sense his mounting impatience by the rattling of its pages. The whole idea had been unpopular with him from the moment I announced my induction. ("You're almost a man already. You got no business at your age with such childish things. You should be learning typing and shorthand so it'll be easier for you when you go to college.") The fact that our troop met weekly at Central United conjured up horrible visions in his mind. He saw me standing in the church pulpit before packed audiences bearing witness of my conversion to their faith and denouncing my own people. I tried to explain that we met in the basement of the building and promised I would never so much as venture upstairs where the pulpit was located. These preliminary explanations and promises he received with a grain of salt. My pre-parade rehearsal did nothing to improve his outlook.

Still he said nothing—until I began rehearsing the Scout oath: "On my honor I promise that I will do my duty to God and the King. . ."

That did it. The newspaper landed half-way across the room as if blown by a hundred-mile-an-hour gale. A split-second later came the thunder.

"Just what in the hell do they think they're doing, making a soldier out of a kid. Look at you, you're not even twelve years old yet."

"Make up your mind," I said. "Last month you told me I was almost a man already. Besides, they're not making a soldier out of me. Honest. Just a Boy Scout."

"As far as I'm concerned a uniform is a uniform, and I don't like it."

"But even bus drivers wear uniforms—"

"Bus drivers don't go around saluting and promising to do their duty to God and the King."

I assured my father that our activities were entirely peace-oriented.

"We learn all sorts of valuable things. How to signal with flags, how to make a fire by rubbing two sticks together, how to make a stretcher to carry somebody with a broken leg."

"That's exactly what they made me learn in the army.

Next thing you know they'll stick a rifle in your hands and tell you to go shoot people."

We argued back and forth for an hour, my father serving, I retrieving. He remained unconvinced. He was remembering his own youth. At the age of nineteen, having failed to rupture himself by deliberately lifting heavy stones (a sort of un-fitness program), he was passed as medically sound and conscripted into the Russian Army. Two years later, his cavalry unit hopelessly bogged down on the Austrian Front, he took stock of his military career, and decided that it had nowhere to go but down. Together with two other Jewish conscripts who had come to the same conclusion, he chose to go sideways. Late one night he and his cohorts demobilized themselves, shedding the Czar's uniform and rifle, and fleeing across the border to Roumania. It was a tale I'd heard often. Historians may have overlooked or ignored it, but I was always a little proud that—almost single-handed—my father made peace with the Kaiser in August of 1917.

Now, barely twenty-one years later, here was the peace-maker's son, not yet in his teens, about to study semaphore, first aid in the field and incendiary techniques.

"Don't worry," I said, "they don't teach anything about war. In fact just the opposite. Tomorrow we're going to church to hear a sermon all about Lord Baden-Powell and scouting."

"Which church?"

"St. John's Anglican."

"St. John's Anglican! That's where they kneel when they pray. I know; I've heard about it. What are you going to do when they kneel down, eh?"

I hadn't thought about that. In the past, when problems of that nature arose, I was always able to fake it. It was easy during morning exercises at school; the others would never notice that my lips didn't move throughout the Lord's Prayer because all heads were bowed and eyes shut tight in the prescribed attitude of piety. In the murmur of thirty young voices asking forgiveness for their trespasses, the silence of one non-Christian trespasser was inconspicuous. When they sang "Jesus Loves Me" I quietly substituted "Moses" for "Jesus" and thanked God that I was never called upon to sing the hymn solo.

But kneeling in church—that was a religious crisis I hadn't faced before. Father was no help. "Those short pants'll sure do you a lot of good. Either you'll freeze your knees off, or you'll skin 'em raw kneeling in the cathedral."

The parade went well. True, there were no spectators (who wants to watch Boy Scouts parading on a cold November Sunday morning?), but at least my hat stayed on and my socks stayed up.

Inside the cathedral now. Sun streaming in through stained glass windows. Dean and Bishop in black and white robes leading the choir in the majestic processional, organ resounding throughout the high gothic-arched sanctuary. A far cry from the second-storey Foresters Hall, reeking of fresh varnish and stale beer, that my congregation rented for religious services until the early forties when the first synagogue was built.

As a courtesy, the Anglicans yielded the front pews to the boys from Central United; thus I had the misfortune to be seated almost directly under the dignified noses of the impressive Dean and the even more impressive Bishop.

And then it came. The moment of truth. The Bishop rose and spread his arms: "Let us pray."

The whole cathedral shifted forward to its knees. I alone sat frozen stiff in my pew not through courage but through fear. I was certain someone would cry aloud "Stop the prayer!" and I would be led off under close arrest to some dungeon deep in the bowels of St. John's, an unwitting Jewish martyr in a High Anglican stronghold.

It seemed the prayer would never end. "Grant in these troubled times Thy blessing upon all our rulers . . ." And there commenced an inventory of all our rulers as of 1938, beginning of course with the Royal Family, and working downward through an inexhaustible list of federal, provincial and municipal statesmen, the judiciary, the armed services and—at the bottom of the list—the most feared public official of all, our Local Chief of Police. At last, "Amen" and the whole cathedral shifted back into its seats and the service continued.

I had stayed put. And I had survived.

The first question fired at me when I returned home was not unexpected.

"Well, soldier, how did you handle yourself when it came to the kneeling business?"

Summoning all the sarcasm that a twelve-year-old boy-man can possess, I shot back with a sneer, "I deserted my troop and skipped across the border."

Then, remembering the Scout motto—"Be Prepared"—I retreated without a moment's delay before the former Russian army man could mount an attack, and sought haven with a friend who lived two safe blocks away. For the remainder of that Sunday, my friend's house was Roumania.

The Salesman

"He's a man way out there in the blue,
riding on a smile and a shoeshine . . . A
salesman is got to dream, boy. It comes with
the territory."
(From *Death of a Salesman* by Arthur Miller, Viking
Press, New York, 1949)

He rode on more than a smile and shoeshine. Much more.
From what I saw of it, his life was crammed full of silver
linings. The lapels of his double-breasted suit were cut
razor-sharp and the three points of his breastpocket handkerchief stood up crisp and white and meticulously spaced.
He travelled in the Pullman club car of the Toronto-Sault
train. He ate steak every night in the best Chinese restaurant
in town. And—most important of all—he quartered himself
on the top floor of the biggest hotel, a nine-storey structure
whose lobby was populated with important-looking men
sitting in leather armchairs reading out-of-town papers and
smoking cigars.

Enveloped as he was in an aura of success, why then, I
wondered, were his periodic descents upon my father's
clothing store greeted with such lack of grace and hospi-
tality?

"Oh, so it's *you* again. What are you selling this time, cancer?"

"Aw c'mon, don't be like that. I've got the greatest winter line you ever laid eyes on. Golden merchandise, every piece!"

"Genius, that's what you said about your fall line. Take a look at my stock of suits. Middle of September already and two-thirds of your golden merchandise is still catching lint here. I can't give it away. The Salvation Army turned it down; even people on relief won't wear it."

"Look, autumn is autumn and winter is winter. You can't expect to sell fall coats in December, can you?"

With this fast bit of verbal footwork the salesman managed to transport my father's economic outlook from the present season to the next. Don't bother to examine the logic; there was none. This was simply the standard opening round of a mating game between two old sea otters: the salesman (male otter) playfully and persistently luring the reluctant clothier (female otter) into the hotel sample-room (the underwater bridal chamber) by a series of deft twists and turns in the waves. At last "the bride" succumbed.

"Alright, I'll look at your line . . . but I won't buy!"

This last threat was, of course, meaningless, a resolution that was always stated for the record at the outset only to dissolve the moment my father was exposed to the latest fashions. He was careful, however, to maintain a cool poker face.

"Hm . . . this little number . . . not great, but not bad. Might just sell—"

"Might! You'll sell 'em by the carload. You'll beg me for repeats. What's-his-name in North Bay bought four dozen of this one number alone."

"Liar, he bought two dozen."

"God should strike me dead, he bought four dozen."

"Two."

"Okay, so maybe it was three dozen."

"You're still a liar, but gimme three dozen anyway."

Having reached this plateau, the salesman, with masterful timing, would suddenly remember a new joke going the rounds in the needle trade on Toronto's Spadina Avenue. The joke (well told, usually in Yiddish so the obscenities would be beyond me) was the oil that lubricated the rest of the day's dealings. With less agony now the remainder of the saleman's winter line found its way onto the order pad. Father was hooked for another season.

It was time now for the salesman to play the game in reverse, to become "the hooked." He would look at my father slyly, cautiously.

"Deal 'em?"

"Deal 'em," my father commanded, and the salesman immediately produced a fresh pack of cards and they began, with great zest, a gin rummy tournament that might last for hours. To my delight, the players needled each other steadily and mercilessly. ("When did you learn to play gin rummy, this morning?" . . . "You should've played that hand with your feet instead of your head, you would've got a better result" . . . "Maybe you got education, but it takes brains, not education, to play this game.") With each triumphant cry of "Gin!" from father, the salesman would smite his own forehead, raise his eyes to heaven, and cry aloud, "My God, this man is slaughtering me!" Finally the victim could bear defeat no longer.

"I need a schnapps. Let's go up to my room."

They drank rye—straight, no ice, no water, no ginger ale—while I drank in the splendid view of the city at dusk from the ninth-floor windows. To the south, the Michigan side of the border, and lake freighters riding high in the water with their holds empty, inching their way through the canal locks and up the St. Mary's River to take on iron ore and grain. To the west, the black, ugly expanse of steel mills spread against an orange sky—mills that belched and hissed and glowed, and poured smoke and the smell of sulphur across the horizon. To the north, dark green hills presided over by the stately Collegiate Institute. To the east, the forbidden territory: Simpson Street with its porched and pillared Local Establishment houses; and just out of sight and beyond the reach of smoke and sulphur, the Golf and Country Club. Other adventurers might find their fortunes by going west, but in this town you hadn't made it until you'd gone east.

I loved this panorama. At this precise moment it was mine, exclusively mine: no other kid in the whole of Sault Ste. Marie—not even a Simpson Street kid—could share this view. This was my reward for having served, during the hours just past, as kibitzer, adviser (usually wrong), waterboy, cigarette-fetcher, window opener and closer, lamplighter, telephone answering service, and for having had the good sense not to laugh at the salesman's joke even though I had a pretty good idea what the Yiddish punchline really meant.

Afterward, as we left the hotel, father counted up his winnings—four, perhaps five, dollars. I was impressed.

"Gee, he must be very rich to be able to lose that kind of money. Every time he comes to town you beat him in rummy."

"He's not very rich. He's very smart. He makes sure I win most of the time. Don't you understand? You never bite the hand that feeds you. Remember that in case—God forbid—you ever become a salesman."

Getting into the car I heard my father grumble, "Ach, it's

a lousy life." His tone was edged in bitterness. I looked up at the ninth floor of the hotel. The salesman was probably ordering dinner from room service, or perhaps he was on his way to the Chinese restaurant for "prime juicy T-bone with golden french fries." A lousy life? Impossible. And I thought, happily: another three months and he'll be back with the spring line, and I'll get to see the view from the ninth floor again.

After all, a boy's got to dream. It comes with the territory.

Café Society

Once again Jimmy Lee, proprietor of the Ritz Café, was in trouble. But this time it was no ordinary trouble such as, say, a complaint of the Health Inspector that the dishwater looked like crankcase oil, or a charge by a freshman constable that Jimmy Lee was serving booze in coffee cups—Jimmy, incidentally, was always careful to serve bootleg rye with cream and sugar on the side. No, this time Jimmy Lee was in real trouble. The trouble centred around one Doris Larue, Jimmy Lee's waitress, and a girl with important connections back in her home town of Blind River, about ninety miles east of the Sault. Six months ago she had been deserted by her lover in one of the booths at the Ritz. It was her first Saturday night in town, and she sat there, this half-starved, half-breed girl, a living bundle of dirty laundry whom no one would want to bother washing. No one but Jimmy Lee, that is. Was it compassion that moved Jimmy Lee to give her shelter that night? Or was it some shrewd perception on his part? Did he, like some mythical prince, look upon this street-scarred female and suddenly realize that under her skin, that had the colour and texture of used sandpaper, lay a princess? Whatever motivated the proprietor of the Ritz was now unimportant, for today Doris, though she still lacked royal quality, no longer looked half-starved. Indeed she had waxed plump, plumper than one would have expected of a girl who—perhaps for the first time in her poor young life—had been exposed to three square meals a day.

One night, with the same absence of pomp and ceremony that had marked her initial appearance at the Ritz, Doris simply disappeared. A day later her important connections arrived from Blind River. They lingered over their coffees toward closing time, watching Jimmy Lee empty his cash register and switch off the electric outdoor sign. Jimmy Lee, not knowing that the last two patrons in the cafe this night were Doris' brothers, called to them, "You finish now, I gotta close up." A moment later all the lights at the Ritz went off, and the restaurateur and his two half-breed patrons punched and struggled in the darkness until Jimmy Lee was unconscious.

The morning after the agony at Jimmy Lee's, I sat in the chair at Jack's Barbershop. My eyes were shut tight as clipped hair fell over my forehead and down my nose, but my ears were opened wide.

"He sure looks like the devil," Jack said, snipping and clipping hair and smacking his lips. Jack's last name was "Apostle" and while he possessed neither the talent nor temperament to cut the Messiah's hair, he did have an air of self-satisfaction and moral righteousness that took the form of lip-smacking. Jack was speaking now of Jimmy Lee's physical condition. "Yep, he sure looks awful. Both eyes black. Jaw looks like one of them U.S. army balloons they got up in the air over the locks."

"Did they get the guys who did it?" I asked.

"Naw, the police ain't gonna bust their behinds on this

sorta thing. Besides, it's natural justice anyway. I always say you should let natural justice take its own course."

"Why did they beat him up?"

Jack halted his scissors in mid-air and reflected for a moment. "Nope," he said, starting to clip again, "I don't think it's my place to tell you, young fella. Maybe you better ask your father. All I can say is, there used to be a law out west that a Chinese guy couldn't hire a white girl to work in his restaurant. They oughta have that law around here, by God!"

"But she wasn't white," I pointed out.

"Don't matter. Point is, she wasn't Chinese. These fellas should stick to their own. They got all sorts of funny ideas, you know."

Apostle smacked his lips, reassuring himself that he was a normal, decent, everyday kind of citizen.

By the time Jack sprinkled a few drops of sweet-smelling water on my scalp and applied the final comb-strokes, two or three neighbouring businessmen had come into his shop. The talk was exclusively about Jimmy Lee. Everyone wondered how he had survived the assault, though no one seemed particularly concerned that the law had been broken, or that Jimmy Lee was a bloodied and bruised victim.

I ran next door to my father's store. "Did you hear what happened to Jimmy Lee last night?" I asked excitedly. "They say that girl's brothers nearly killed him. They say he really had it coming, too."

"Who said?" my father asked, looking up at me from his desk.

"All the men at Jack's Barbershop—"

"All the men at Jack's Barbershop said that, eh?"

"Uh huh."

My father frowned angrily and returned to the papers on his desk.

"Bastards," he muttered. "Every one of them bastards."

Was my father really in sympathy with Jimmy Lee? If he was, then he was very much alone for I, too, sided with the majority. There was no point in arguing with my father. He had his feelings, which only he understood. And I had mine. It never occurred to me that there might be another side to the story. Even if there were, I wouldn't have cared. Secretly I was glad the Brothers Larue had beaten Jimmy Lee. I thought: now, if only they would set fire to the Ritz Café, and burn it right down to the ground!

If the Ritz Café had a reason to exist, it certainly wasn't the food, nor was it the atmosphere.

On Sundays the big special at the Ritz was cream of to-mato soup. All other days of the week the soup-du-jour was home-made vegetable, a pale orange-coloured liquid in whose depths there lurked, like a submarine, a long, slender slice of carrot that surfaced when agitated by a spoon, menac-ing any odd pea or bean that happened to be floating in the vicinity. Seven days of the week Jimmy Lee's menu—always announced, never printed—featured "loose beef" and "ahpoh pie," the former invariably over-done under a small lake of brown gravy, the latter invariably baked with tinned apples that tasted more of tin than apple.

I doubt that Jimmy Lee ever heard of César Ritz after whom this restaurant was named; in all likelihood the place received its name in the same manner Jimmy Lee had re-ceived his—offhandedly, on the spur of the moment. Years before, in Vancouver, Jimmy Lee had stood wide-eyed and open-mouthed before an immigration officer who was shout-ing something at him that made no sense at all, partly be-cause Jimmy Lee—lately of Canton—understood not a word of

English, partly because his comrades of the voyage—those who had shared steerage with him for what seemed an eternity—were confusing him, jabbering excitedly in Chinese and shoving, eager to press well inland lest the new country should suddenly disconnect itself from the wharf and leave them to drift helplessly back across the Pacific. Finally, the uniformed officer, bored by the repetition of his routine questions, impatient at the inability of the Chinese to answer them, hastily scrawled a note on a slip of government paper. "Okay," he said, thrusting the paper at the young man from Canton, "your name's Jimmy Lee, remember that. Next!"

As for the name "Ritz Café," perhaps Jimmy Lee had seen it somewhere on the long journey from Vancouver to Sault Ste. Marie. More likely it was suggested to him by the town's commissioner of business licences, the same municipal official who was responsible for creating such imaginative trade names as "Bellevue Hotel," "Peerless Laundry," "Royal Shoe Repair."

Seasons came and went without much effect upon the Ritz Café. Its windows were always streaked with steam so that even in July the place appeared to be flushed and sweating with a mid-winter fever. Inside, untouched by the sun, stood two rows of booths constructed of plywood, varnished and revarnished, wiped occasionally with a dry greasy cloth when the crumbs and ketchup drippings became intolerable even by Jimmy Lee's sub-basement standards.

Understandably, the Ritz Café hardly attracted the town's elite. Even American tourists, whose hunger for steak after a grinding day on Canadian roads often blinded them to life's finer amenities, sensed immediately upon venturing into the Ritz Café that they had blundered. Heeling sharply about like soldiers in training, they retreated to the sidewalk, scratching their heads in wonderment that such a vast dichotomy could exist between place and placename.

Jimmy Lee's clientele, accordingly, was drawn from the lowest rung of the Sault's social ladder. In fact, the lowest rungs of many other communities' social ladders regularly sent representatives to the Ritz Café. Just about every itinerant drunk or vagrant—in that brief downhill interval between his arrival in town and his incarceration in the District jail—found his way to one of the booths at Jimmy Lee's. There the visitor would flop, unwilling or unable to pay for his toast and coffee, cursing and muttering at his Cantonese host, ignoring Jimmy Lee's screamed protests, until the black police Plymouth drew up to transport him to the lockup.

By far the largest group of patrons at the Ritz Café were the Indians and half-breeds who drifted in and out of town: people without destinations, aimless, surly, their mackinaw jackets smelling like damp sawdust—they found no welcome whatsoever in the town's first-rate eating establishments and very little welcome in the second-rate ones; they therefore settled for the third-rate, namely Jimmy Lee's. But it was not at all a friendly settlement. Food and money were always traded grudgingly; only scorn was exchanged with any generosity. Often—particularly on Saturday nights when cheap wine had been flowing in back alleys and behind billboards and the Indians were of a mood to dance in the aisle between the two rows of booths while the jukebox blared the saga of "The Wabash Cannonball"—Jimmy Lee would decide that money wasn't everything in this world and, throwing open the front door of the restaurant, he would order his stomping, whooping patrons to cavort the hell out. Inevitably they refused. Inevitably there drew up two black police Plymouths, causing the night revelers to scatter, some retiring meekly to their booths, others escaping into Queen

Street, while a handful of obstreperous customers were es-
corted like naughty schoolboys into the rear seats of the
Plymouths.

There were two other steady patrons of the Ritz in those
days—my father and I. We lived in an apartment over my
father's store, directly across the street from the café. My
mother had died some years earlier, and my stepmother lay
dying in the hospital. There was now no woman in our
household, and so my father and I found it easier to take
most of our meals in restaurants. As one might expect in a
small town, the range of eateries was limited, dominated by
Chinese and Italians, footsore sallow-complexioned men who
found their ways from the Orient and the Mediterranean to
this glorious land of golden french fries. We knew every
menu in town by heart, even the freshly-typed menu at the
Windsor Hotel where we ate in style once in a while when
my father was feeling flush and had a desire for a crisp white
tablecloth and a certain pink-skinned Finnish waitress.

We ate frequently at Jimmy Lee's mainly because it was
there. It was, after all, the handiest café in town on a foul
winter night. And it was cheap; a full-course steak dinner
cost a mere forty-five cents (except on Sundays when the
cream of tomato soup drove the prix fixe all the way up to
fifty cents). Nevertheless, I loathed the Ritz; detested the
drifters who slouched and slobbered in the neighbouring
booths, the stained cutlery, the glasses marked with strange
fingerprints and filled with cloudy water, the Soo Dairy cal-
endar on the wall portraying a lazy-eyed jersey cow, the am-
bient tension whenever a drunk suddenly stumbled into the
restaurant and slid clumsily into a booth shouting, "Hey,
magahai! Gimme somethin' t'eat, right away, y'hear."

I had no particular affection for Jimmy Lee either, for that matter. His manner with me was distant and abrupt most of the time. "What you want, boy?" was his standard greeting, and after that my orders were accepted, executed and delivered without further conversation. I could have choked on a chicken bone, drowned in my soup, keeled over from a sudden attack of ptomaine poisoning; it wouldn't have mattered a damn to Jimmy Lee. I was "boy," a face in the gloom that consumed loose beef and ahpoh pie and left a quarter and two dimes beside the cash register on the way out. In other restaurants on Queen Street it was different. Vic, an ancient Chinese who operated "The Savoury," liked to discuss the war and the economy with me and constantly pumped me about my father's current wins and losses on the stock market. Carmen, at the "Adanac Grill," would tell me about the way his "old lady" used to make spaghetti. Herman, who named his fish-and-chip shop after himself, was a frustrated piano player and we conversed about music over the roar and sputter of his deep-fryer. But with Jimmy Lee it was "What you want, boy?" Nothing more.

"I hate this place," I would say to my father time and time again as we sat waiting for Jimmy Lee's infamous vegetable soup. "I hate the place, the people in it, and I don't like him either. Besides, I can tell he can't stand me. Why do we always have to eat here?" I knew the answer of course, but it was important for me to sound off, to reject my surroundings, declare my superiority to all of it, preserve my self-respect. My father never bothered to reply in detail. "Don't worry about Jimmy Lee; he's just as much a mensch as any of us." That was all he would say.

That assertion was always too much for me to swallow. "How can you call him a mensch? Some mensch!"

I was referring, with contempt borrowed from other and older people in the neighbourhood, to Jimmy Lee's mode of living. Jimmy Lee was—as far as anyone knew—a bachelor. There were tales that he had deserted a wife and children back in Canton, which tales of course were never substantiated. There were other tales too: that Jimmy Lee slept with various Indian and half-breed women who worked as waitresses at the Ritz, sullen maidens in their late teens and beer-swollen matrons in their forties whom he allegedly lured into his room at the rear of the restaurant with cash and other forms of largesse. These tales, too, went unproved. Still, from time to time, small shreds of evidence suggested that the management's relations with his serving staff didn't simply begin and end in the public area of the Ritz. Why would Jimmy Lee purchase expensive silk stockings from my father's store? Why, on occasion, a dress or chenille housecoat? Who knew? The point was that whatever contact Jimmy Lee had with the female world was loveless and ephemeral. That much was plain to everyone. The clothing merchants along the block, the druggist, the barber, the manager of the liquor store—everybody gossiped about Jimmy Lee with a mixture of amusement and disgust. "Whenever you see him with his hand in his pocket," one of them quipped, "it's because he's either deciding to screw the government or screw a squaw." In the community's eyes Jimmy Lee was a lecher preying upon Indian and half-breed females who appeared and disappeared like weeds.

My father, to be honest about it, joined in much of the public speculation about Jimmy Lee's nefarious deeds, though with less relish than his colleagues along that stretch of Queen Street. But to me, privately, it was always the same protestation: "Don't worry about Jimmy Lee; he's just as much a mensch as any of us."

At the time, I wondered what there was about Jimmy Lee that inspired such unaccustomed tolerance in my father. I say "unaccustomed" because my father was never exactly the country's leading advocate of liberty, equality and fraternity. On the subject of his native land—Russia—he was patently schizophrenic. The land itself he loved passionately. ("You think this is a watermelon? Poof! You should see the watermelons we grew in Russia!") But the natives who inhabited that land he hated with equal passion. ("Brutes, ignoramuses, give 'em vodka and pogroms, that's all they're good for.")

Though he paid little more than lip service to his own religion, he took great delight in mocking Christians. On Sunday mornings he would turn up the church-service broadcast on the radio to full volume and join the local Baptists in "Onward Christian Soldiers," marching up and back across the kitchen with a broom, singing the hymn in a high, tremulous falsetto, and eventually collapsing himself (and me) with raucous laughter. Then, suddenly, while I was still laughing, he would frown fiercely and, pointing an angry finger at the radio, would declare between clenched teeth, "Goyim! Listen to the sons-of-bitches, not a mensch among the whole goddam bunch."

His strongest venom was reserved for Polish Jews. It was his contention—based upon "all my years of experience"— that on mankind's scale of goodness and uprightness they, the Polish Jews, ranked at zero. "Never trust a Polock"— again the angry finger, the clenched teeth—"they're the lowest, the shrewdest, and they'll cut your kishkes out for a nickel!"

As for his views about physical appearance, the "Rules and Regulations" read as follows: freckles were a sign of impurity and careless personal hygiene; clear white skin only was acceptable in good social circles. Height was a sign of authority and portliness a symbol of prosperity; therefore, little was to be gained by association with short, skinny people. Small eyes spaced narrowly apart indicated a sneaky personality but a person with large wide eyes could be trusted with your last dollar. He also disliked red hair, dark skin, and any kind of deformity. There were, of necessity, occasional exceptions to the rules; after all, he couldn't live in a vacuum, allowing in from time to time only those who met his requirements. One had to bend one's rules to make a living and to get along socially. Privately he would express to me his distaste for someone who represented a deviation from his standards. "Did you see the freckles on her arms? . . . Did you notice how every rib sticks out on his body? . . . Pheh!"

So much for racial and physical characteristics. When it came to economic status, it may be observed that his own years of struggle, and the universal hard times of the thirties, had not mellowed his outlook. It wasn't a case of his merely disliking poverty; the fact is he wasn't particularly fond of the poor either. Schleppers—the Jewish word for people who lag behind, who have no sense of style, who are losers—is the designation he gave to the poor. Give him the company of overdogs anytime. Only the smell of success was welcome in his nostrils.

It was a lucky thing for mankind that God chose not to delegate to my father the task of designing and manufacturing the human race. The product that would have emerged from his assembly line would have resembled Henry Ford's early masterpieces—one model, one colour, and no substitutes.

Why then such forbearance for Jimmy Lee, a man who met none of my father's rules and regulations? Was there something in common between them, some thin thread that tied them together in this world? Except for the fact that my father landed in Halifax, he and Jimmy Lee had arrived in Canada more or less in the same fashion—penniless, without influence or benefactors, completely mystified by the English language. But what was so extraordinary about that? In that same manner other "untouchables" had arrived: the freckled, the short and skinny, the Polish Jews, the schleppers, the swarthy and dark-skinned of Europe and Asia; yet he showed *them* no special understanding, offered *them* no special clemency.

No, whatever invisible bond joined these two men had nothing at all to do with social and economic causes and effects. It had to do with one thing, and one thing only: women.

As a conscript in the Russian army, my father had left behind in Odessa a girl to whom he had become bethrothed shortly before his induction. From her photographs in our family album, it was obvious she fulfilled his criteria of beauty; moreover, she had a bosom that was ample enough to comfort a regiment. But she troubled him, for inside her handsome head was a lively brain that nourished itself on poetry and politics and philosophy. Not for her the customary domestic prisons in which other young Jewish women willingly incarcerated themselves—the kitchens, the nurseries, the sewing circles. Nor would she hold her tongue in the company of men, dutifully serving them poppyseed cookies and glasses of tea and then resuming her place in the corner like a fixture until summoned forth to serve again. She thought freely, but worse still, she spoke out freely. This trait especially jarred her soldier-lover. As the youngest child of his large family, my father had been the favoured, pampered by his mother, protected by his older sisters, doted upon by his father. He was a small sun around whom the lesser planets of his family circulated worshipfully. But this young woman had a solar system of her own; she was not likely to go into orbit around him.

At last he wrote her from a battlefront station in Austria. "I don't know which is more difficult, to face the enemy in the trenches, or to write this letter, but I have decided that we are so far apart in so many ways . . ." He realized, he wrote, that the letter amounted to a breach of promise to marry. What would she demand by way of compensation? In due course the girl's rabbi replied in her behalf. The girl was grief-stricken, to be sure. "Nevertheless," the rabbi added in the same breath, "her grief is capable of being compensated, praise be to God!"

It required as many rubles as my father could lay hands on—and then some—and it is a fair assumption that a goodly portion of that sum found its way into the rabbi's purse by way of commission. Within a month a document arrived, written in a small, fine Hebrew hand. "You are hereby for- ever and completely released and forgiven," the girl's spirit- ual representative began, ending several hundred words later with "Praise be to God!" Praise be to God, indeed; one good release deserves another, my father said to him- self. And with that, one night when the battlefront was momentarily calm, he released himself forever and com- pletely from the Russian army. Goodbye Russia. He would never look eastward again, except to pray or to watch the morning sun. He was off, heading westward in search of peace, the good life, and the perfect woman.

These he found in Winnipeg, Manitoba. Or thought he found.

The year was 1926. He was a boarder in the home of a
tailor on Selkirk Street, teaching Hebrew to unenthusiastic
little Jewish boys, striving himself to remain above water
in the endless swamps of the English language, earning just
enough coin of the realm to pay for his lodging and keep a
shine on his shoes. The girl this time was the older sister
of one of his pupils. Born in England, she barely spoke a
word of Yiddish, knew absolutely no Hebrew, and knew
nothing about Russia except that Russian Jews ate great
quantities of herring which they brought home wrapped in
damp newspapers from fish markets. This young woman
was no Russian-style beauty, far from it. Still, she had great
appeal: clear skin, soft, wide-spaced eyes, a quiet voice,
genteel manners. Her English was, of course, excellent. In
fact, she was secretary to a member of the Manitoba legis-
lature. Her father's credentials were just about impeccable
too: born in Russia, well-educated in Talmud, once Reeve
of West Kildonan, after that a magistrate, a man of property
and some political influence in the city.

She found her suitor to be a bit of a dandy; he wiped the
dust from the toes of his shoes by rubbing them along the
backs of his trouser-legs from time to time as they strolled
along Portage Avenue; he checked his pencil-stripe moustache regularly in the reflections in shop windows; to avoid
creases, he always unbuttoned his jacket and gave a slight
tug at the knees of his pants when he sat.

A good deal of the time she didn't understand the greenhorn Hebrew teacher. Often he would grope for the right
English expression and come up with something that was
entirely out of context. When that happened the poor girl
would try bravely to suppress laughter, but occasionally her
best efforts failed and he would shake his head from side to
side, impatient with himself, offended by her laughter, frus-

trated by the language of the land. And yet she was in-
trigued by this strange greenhorn because he was so different
from the local young men. He traded Hebrew quotations
with her father, matched the older man proverb for proverb,
shone at family gatherings with the older relatives who regarded his yeshiva education as a prime attribute in life.
There was a kind of old country quaintness about his manners with women—shy and formal publicly, ardent privately,
always to some degree a poseur.

At the appointed hour of their wedding he walked with
military bearing down the aisle toward the chupah, this
greenhorn thousands of miles removed from his natural
habitat, in possession of nothing by way of assets save his
high aspirations, his energy, and the carefully pressed suit
on his back. She walked down the same aisle a moment later,
a woman very much living within her natural habitat but
doing a strange thing. As they turned to face each other
under the wedding canopy, each must inwardly have asked:
what am I doing here?

A few weeks after their marriage he discovered a letter she
had written to a girlfriend. "He's not much to look at and
has no money to speak of," she confided, "but he made love
like a caveman and I guess I simply caved in . . ." How did
that letter come to be left exposed to view? Did she intend
him to see it? What possessed him to eavesdrop on her secret
communications? No matter; the letter was never mailed.
Instead my father confiscated it and thereafter it remained
among his most private papers where, like a malignant
tumour, it grew and grew, spreading its incurable cancer
throughout the heart and limbs of their relationship.

Everything about my father's Great Canadian Dream now
began to turn sour. Perhaps it was that fatal letter, perhaps
it was the similarity in personality between bridegroom and

father-in-law, a case of like forces repelling after a brief, initial attraction. Perhaps it was the immediate proximity of my mother's large family, with its ubiquitous aunts and uncles and cousins, that threatened to strangle the newly-weds. What the marriage seemed to call for was a change of venue, a fresh start in a fresh locale.

The fresh locale became a bed-sitting room with a kitchen-ette and shared toilet at the rear of a secondhand furniture store on Queen Street in Sault Ste. Marie, operated by a Ukrainian and his fat, good-natured wife. But the fresh start —the rekindling of the old flame, or the kindling of a new flame—had yet to occur. Gone from sight and sound were the ever-present relatives, the domineering father-figure, but still there was the letter . . . always the letter. The cramped confines of the bed-sitting room that might have drawn them closer to each other only served to broaden the distances between them. Each day they discovered in those poor surroundings less and less to rejoice in.

In 1927—the year Lindbergh crossed the Atlantic and gave birth to trans-oceanic flight—my father crossed his own Atlantic—that vast and stormy space that separated him from his wife—and nine months later I was born.

If, in the magical moment of insertion that spawned me, my father and mother shared any faint notion they were creating a bond that would unite them indestructibly, they were woefully mistaken. It quickly became apparent that my arrival on the scene was precisely what that union didn't need! Not only were three a crowd in those quarters behind the secondhand store, but the third occupant wailed day and night, so much so that at last the fat, good-natured Ukrainian landlady knocked on the door and said, hesitantly, "Please missus, you understand, my man and me getting too old . . ." and it was time to find a new bed-sitting room somewhere in

Sault Ste. Marie.

What was more serious was that my birth had aggravated my mother's pre-existing kidney problem so that it now took on all the pains and attendant fears of a full-scale disease.

Then came the days of total struggle—the mid-thirties; struggle to survive the barebone days of the Depression and keep the small clothing business afloat, struggle on my mother's part with the ever-increasing agony of her kidney disease, struggle on my father's part to pay for the doctors and medications her condition demanded, struggle on the part of both husband and wife to find some logical answer to the question "What am I doing here?" that nagged each of them from that first terrifying moment under the chupah.

In the end my mother's sickness defeated them both.

The afternoon of July 12, 1936, was so hot in Winnipeg that a newspaper reporter was photographed frying an egg on the sidewalk at the corner of Main and Portage. Five miles from downtown, in a cemetery in West Kildonan, on that blistering day, my mother was buried. We sat shiva in my grandparents' living quarters over their grocery store. The windows were opened as wide as they would open and electric fans had been placed near the windowsills. Humming steadily in the prairie heat, the fans blew out of that stuffy apartment the smells of gift roses and salmon sandwiches, and Part One of my father's Great Canadian Dream.

Part Two began a year later precisely where Part One ended—in Winnipeg. I had spent the year after my mother's death living with my grandparents in West Kildonan while my father carried on with life in Sault Ste. Marie. "It's no way to live," his friends told him. "You must find yourself another wife." Everyone knew one woman or another who was just right for a widower in his early forties and for his skinny, bespectacled ten-year old. The most impressive candidate turned out to be a Winnipeg school teacher of thirty-five. A spinster, she was pleasant-faced, lively, articulate, and had a good figure. I was particularly impressed because she owned an Auburn sedan with headlights the size of full moons. One day, in the Auburn, she said to me, "How would you like me to be your new mother?" "Fine," I responded instantly. This was the final seal of approval; we celebrated, she and I, over hamburgers at a drive-in stand. Soon after, she left Winnipeg for Sault Ste. Marie to marry my father. I was to follow her right after their honeymoon, and I began counting the days until my return to my old room, my old school, my old friends. Several weeks passed, a month, two months, and more. I began to complain: what was taking so long? Not until six full months had gone by was I sent for.

I stood beside my old bed unpacking. My new stepmother stood in the open doorway of my room, smiling, asking me questions about the two-day journey by train, enjoying each boyish observation about my trip east as if it contained some enormous pearl of wisdom. My father appeared in the doorway. Smiling still, she looked up at him and touched his face with her hand. He turned his face away brusquely, at the same time pushing her hand aside. Her smile froze. Quickly she looked over at me as if to say, "It's really nothing, it's all right, everything is all right."

Late that night, as I lay in bed unscrambling memories of past nights and speculating about future days, I heard the sound of voices coming from the office at the rear of my father's store, which was directly beneath my bedroom.

"You must go back to Winnipeg."

"I can't go back to Winnipeg."

"But I don't want you here. I didn't want you here from

the first minute."

"I can never face all those people again."

"I don't give a goddam what you've got to face. I can't stand the sight of you in my house anymore. Just get the hell out of my life."

"I'll kill myself before I go back."

"Then kill yourself!"

It was the first of many such bitter dialogues I was to overhear following my return home. They quarrelled—he raging, she pleading—in every forum and on every occasion imaginable. No one knew precisely the cause for all this enmity; everyone fell back upon trite, empty observations: "Second marriages are just repeats of first marriages only everything is worse; they never work out." Or, referring to my father: "You know Russians—stubborn, hot-tempered, always painting life and themselves black." Or, referring to his second wife: "She's a big-city girl; maybe she expected something better; she really had nothing in common with him to begin with." Volunteer marriage counsellors sprang into service everywhere. Had they been professionals—trained, skilled, experienced—it is doubtful that their resources would have been up to the task. As amateurs, relying upon mere guess-work and old-country gut feelings, they failed miserably and often only inflamed the situation by siding with the weaker of the contenders, my stepmother.

Three years and hundreds of battles later, she lay hospitalized, suffering from colitis. Gravely, her doctor shook his head. "It was bound to happen," he told my father. "Nobody's system can stand that much constant anxiety and aggravation . . ." My father, noting the implied accusation, added the physician to his blacklist. Her condition grew worse, his blacklist lengthened; the doctor eventually moved up on the list until he occupied the top position. It was as if my stepmother had conspired with this medicine man to torture my father's conscience and drain his finances at the same time. After each nightly visit to her hospital bedside—a short, dutiful attendance during which few words or gestures were ever exchanged—my father would recite what became in time an unvarying catechism of hate: "Why did I ever come to America? I must have been out of my mind . . . Why did I need another woman? Enemies, that's who talked me into it . . . What did I do to deserve this? There must be a devil in my life."

This went on for months while my stepmother grew weaker and thinner, and still there were no clues as to how it all began, only the never-ending flow of my father's self-pity and vituperations. I began to pray that she would die.

But she did not die. In the hospital room, that smelled of ether and starchy bed-linen and human waste, she hung on, becoming yellowish and staring blankly at the ceiling.

One evening, in the autumn, instead of the expected catechism came an unexpected news bulletin: "They think she should go to Winnipeg," my father said, pulling out of the hospital driveway as he always did, quickly, almost impetuously. "There's a specialist there . . ." A few days later, I saw her off. Because the train trip from Sault Ste. Marie was an arduous stop-and-start affair, it was decided that she should travel by passenger steamship to the lakehead, thence to Winnipeg by train. She was put aboard the ship on a stretcher, and my father went aboard with her. A minute later he was back in the car and we drove away, I turning to look at the ship which remained still moored at the dock. I looked at my father. His face was stone-gray. "Aren't we going to wait until the boat leaves?" I asked. "What the hell for? That's how she came, and that's how she's going, and that's all there is to it," he said, barely moving his lips.

"What do you mean?" "Never mind. It's not important." I looked back as we drove along Bay Street and up Elgin. Only the red, white and black funnel was still visible.

Winter came early that year. By Armistice Day the lawns in front of the Court House were covered with a foot of snow and the long, plaintive notes of "The Last Post" cracked and wavered, one moment loud, the next moment distant, in a wind that blew from all four directions at once. The following week the storekeepers along Queen Street began to unpack cartons of Christmas decorations that had spent ten months in the dampness and dust of their cellars; decorations that looked like used greeting cards, weary greens and faded reds of lifeless streamers, shrivelled tinsel, water-stained posters wishing one and all a Merry Xmas, reminding mankind that it was time once again to celebrate the birth of "X". It was an annual commercial ritual, performed without any apparent trace of spiritual energy by the men and women of the shops. Yet, there was a kind of bravery and optimism about it. It would have been so natural, in that heartless November of 1941, as one arose in the morning to the bad news from Europe and Asia, and looked out the window at the bad news in the sky and in the streets, to say, "To hell with it, to hell with everything;" so natural to crawl back into bed and hide under the blankets hoping that by the time the day had arrived at its fullest light, the world would have gone away, far far away. Instead, the town dressed itself for Christmas, turned on its strings of coloured street lights, somehow forced a smile on its face for the yuletide season.

Everywhere, that is, except at the Ritz Café.

If that restaurant showed few effects from the changing

seasons, it showed none at all from the changing moods of man. It mattered less than a palmful of salt to the management and staff, and to most of the clientele of the Ritz Café, that battles were being lost and won overseas, that hopes were being dimmed and awakened at home, that people were determined at all costs to pretend that there was peace and goodwill mixed in with the blood and mud of war.

Besides, Jimmy Lee had his own problems to worry about concerning the Larue affair.

Jimmy Lee's multiple contusions and swellings had put an end to the casualness with which his neighbours regarded the goings-on at the Ritz. Perhaps such activities were, after all, a serious threat to the good order of the neighbourhood. Perhaps there was a profoundly sordid side to Jimmy Lee's affairs with his waitresses that might tend to deprave the populace and should be expurgated from the Christmassy streets lest it pollute and ruin this holy season. Perhaps the storekeepers on the block resented the fact that they—Christian and Jew alike—took the trouble to adorn their establishments with the required festive trappings, while Jimmy Lee sold his vegetable soup by the gallon and his roast beef by the hundredweight and spent not so much as a penny in the observance of Christ's miraculous arrival. Whatever the reasons, Jimmy Lee's neighbours whispered into life a quiet campaign to get the Ritz Café closed.

The anti-Ritz conspirators met twice daily during the morning and afternoon coffee breaks at Herman's Grill, and for the time being the usual business gossip was suspended. Like stockmarkets that rise and fall upon the temporary indigestion of a single president or prime minister, the fortunes of Queen Street had suddenly become highly sensitive to the amorous entanglements of a single Chinese restaurateur. The selling of shoes and hammers and cough syrup and haircuts depended upon the eradication of the Ritz Café and the particular brand of society who ate—and did other things—therein. In the booths at Herman's, pointed questions were asked in low but very determined voices. "What about calling in the Sanitation Inspector?" ... "Isn't this sort of thing under the control of the Health Department?" ... "Maybe we should consult old Doc Gimby, the M.O.H.?" ..."Couldn't the clergymen in this area get together and put some pressure on Council?"

Throughout these deliberations my father sat silent, careful not to commit himself to any plan designed to rid the block of the Ritz Café, but at the same time just as careful not to defend Jimmy Lee, at least openly. So nobody really knew how my father felt about the subject of Jimmy Lee's thornlike presence—nobody except me. To me my father confided his attitude about Jimmy Lee, an attitude that hadn't changed a fraction despite all the ugly stories. It was still: "Don't worry about Jimmy Lee, he's just as much a mensch as any of us."

And then—a few days before Christmas—the moment of truth arrived.

A group of storekeepers sat in a booth at Herman's stirring their coffee. "Hey, look at Harry," one of the group said, pointing to the man who had just come into the restaurant and was approaching them. "Looks like he's ready to commit murder."

Harry, who sold hardware a few doors down the street from the Ritz, came over to the booth and sat down without removing his overcoat.

"Do you know what that bastard Chinaman has gone and done now?" he asked, his voice quivering with anger. "He's gone and thrown out that nice little lady from the Salvation Army. You know, the one that goes around collecting at

Christmas. Practically tossed her out on her ass and yelled at her that if she ever came into the place again he'd take a butcher knife to her."

"My God!"

"The sonofabitch!"

"That's gotta be the last straw!"

Still shaking, Harry pressed on, determined to take advantage of his audience's outrage. "I say we should call the police and lay some kind of a charge against him. That's gotta be assault, isn't it? I tried to get the Salvation Army woman to do it, but they're so goddam full of charity. So I say it's up to us."

One by one the other men voiced their agreement. But when it came my father's turn to speak up, he looked straight at Harry.

"Why did he throw her out, Harry?"

Harry stared at my father. "Now how the hell would I know? I wasn't there when it happened. Anyway, what's it matter? The point is, he was abusive and threatened her. If you could've seen the look on her face when she came into my shop, you wouldn't give a damn why he threw her out. No sir, you'd just want to go straight into the Ritz and punch the bugger right in the mouth, just like those Indians did."

"Then why didn't you?"

"Why didn't I what?"

"Go straight in there and punch him in the mouth? I mean, if you were that upset."

Harry twisted one side of his mouth into an expression of contempt. Without looking at my father again, he spoke to the others. "Will somebody please tell our friend here that maybe that sort of thing's okay where he and his pal across the street come from but——"

Before Harry could utter another word, he found himself

drenched in coffee. It trickled down his forehead and cheeks and chin onto the front of his overcoat where it soaked into the heavy wool fibres forming massive blotches. The coffee had come from my father's cup which caromed across the table and landed on the floor breaking into several pieces. At the sound of the crashing coffee cup, Herman came running from behind the soda fountain, a wet towel clutched in one hand.

"For Godsakes," he cried, looking at the mess on the floor and shaking his head. "What do you think this is, the Ritz?"

My father held a telegram in his hand. "They think she's dying, I've got to go and make arrangements."

He was speaking of my stepmother as he did always, flatly and without emotion. I had come home from school to find him packing a few things in a small club bag.

"Is that all you're taking?" I asked, nodding toward the couple of shirts and some toiletries in the bag.

"I won't need more than that. I intend to get it all over with one-two-three. Just like that. One-two-three and good-bye once and for all." He snapped the club bag shut. "Come say goodbye at the station. We don't have much time."

On the way to the station he mumbled, "Just my luck. Right in the middle of stocktaking." It was late January, 1942, the sacred time of year when a merchant communed with his inventory, fingering each ticketed garment, and wondering whether it would still be around a year from now.

On the fifth night after his departure for Winnipeg, he returned. I had heard no news whatsoever; indeed, I had no idea when he would return. I was in the kitchen of our apartment, doing my homework, listening to the snow rattle against the skylight over my head. Suddenly the apartment door opened and my father was home. I rose to greet him but could think of nothing more appropriate to say than "You're home."

He put down his club bag. "Sit down," he said, "I have something to tell you." We sat at the kitchen table.

"She's dead. She died before I got there. I took care of the funeral and came back here on the first train I could get. And now I think it's time you knew something. We were never married. Everybody thought we went away and got married in Detroit after she came here from Winnipeg. Well, we did go to Detroit, but the truth is, never got married. I think you are old enough now to understand the reason why. You see, she came here by boat from Port Arthur—the same god-dammed boat that took her away, as a matter of fact—and I was all dressed up fit to kill—new suit and all—to meet her. I was like a young bridegroom, that's how anxious I was to see her and to have her here. But when the boat pulls in toward the dock, I see she's standing at the rail and there's some smart-looking guy standing beside her with his arm around her, and they're smiling at me and laughing, and smiling and laughing at each other. He didn't get off here; he was on his way to Toronto. But when she's finally off the boat I ask her 'Who's the fellow who was with you?' and she says they were once friends when she was teaching school in Portage La Prairie. 'From the looks of it, you must have been awfully good friends' I say to her, because I'm burning up a little. Anyway, it turns out that they were more than just friends. And I knew then, that very second, that I didn't want her anymore. She wasn't. . . do you know what a virgin is?"

"I'm not sure. I guess I know; yes."

"Well she wasn't a virgin. Understand?"

"Yes."

"And I wanted a virgin. I didn't want somebody else's secondhand merchandise. I was entitled to a virgin. It was coming to me. You understand, don't you?"

He paused, waiting for me to agree.

"Yes."

"That same day I told her 'I can't go through with it and I want you to go back to Winnipeg' and she said she'd rather jump into the St. Mary's River than face the trip back to Winnipeg. I offered her money—anything—if she'd leave, but she insisted she really loved me and wanted to be your mother. You know what common-law is? Well, that's how we lived, common-law. Nobody else knows the truth about us. Do you understand what I'm saying to you?"

"Yes."

I said nothing more, just sat staring at the top of the kitchen table, remembering—of all things—that it had been a long time since I'd seen a family-size bottle of Kik.

Passover came in mid-March and with it came invitations for seder meals from solicitous housewives—invitations my father dreaded because they were invariably tinged with rachmonas; moreover he felt compelled to reciprocate and this created a burden. In the past, though he would have preferred to decline, he usually did the graceful thing and accepted, often disclosing after the meal in the privacy of our car that he felt as if he was choking with every mouthful. But this time, he turned down every caller. The caller would plead, "But it's Pesach! You can't eat in a restaurant on Pesach. It's just not right." "Thank you," he would reply, forcing himself to be polite, "it's really so kind of you to be concerned, but my son and I have made arrangements . . ."

I had nothing whatever to do with the arrangements, of course; my father made them all, such as they were. On the first night of Passover—a night that was rainy and foggy—we dined across the street at the Ritz Café. It was a seder night different from all other seder nights in my memory. My father excused me from the traditional Four Questions ("Wherefor is this night distinguished from all other nights of the year?") ; Jimmy Lee's one ritual query ("What you gonna have?") sufficed.

There were no more Doris Larues in Jimmy Lee's life now; various local armies of righteousness had combined forces to see to that. Assisted by his recently-hired helper, a Chinese by the name of George who looked as though he had just completed one life sentence at hard labour and was about to begin a second, Jimmy Lee served this Passover meal.

Instead of matzohs we ate soda biscuits; Jimmy Lee's watery vegetable soup was the broth of our affliction; his apple pie—just as tinny-tasting as ever—our bitter herb, reminding us of the days when our people were slaves in Egypt.

From that Passover on, neither my father nor Jimmy Lee lived again with a woman. From that Passover on, under an arrangement unconsciously made between them, the Chinese restaurateur and the Jewish merchant became the inhabitants of a common desert, each retiring to his private sand dune, prepared in mind and body to survive there, if necessary, for the next forty years.

Press Pressure

So much has been written about the strength and influence of the Jewish mother that one is left with the impression that the Jewish father was nothing more than a grayish bug of a man who left his droppings—a bit of seed here, a bit of cash there—and vanished into some obscure corner of the family fabric; in life, a vague shadow; in death, the occupant of the rearmost provinces of his children's memories, recalled for twenty minutes annually with the burning of a candle and the mumbling of a prayer.

No doubt there existed such mediocrities at the head of Jewish families. But they must have existed in some other part of the country, or perhaps on some other continent. Never in our town. In our town the father—in his house or in his store—was boss. If and when it pleased him, but only if it pleased him, he would condescend to share his throne with his wife; yet at all times he was the eminence, and on or off the throne he held his household in a firm grip.

There were few distractions for the father in those days; service clubs and golf and politics were strictly Gentile pursuits. Father could therefore be counted on to be at home for lunch (which was called dinner) and for dinner (which was called supper) , and if business was a little slow, he could often be counted on to come home for an afternoon nap. Since home was usually an apartment over a store, or a dwelling a mere block or two away, father could also respond promptly to a summons if things got out of hand on the domestic scene. Being his own boss, he didn't have to ask anyone for time off when such emergencies arose.

Fathers came in two varieties: Variety Number One was the benevolent (and sometimes malevolent) despot, a self-appointed governor-general who ruled by vocal decrees—issued frequently and loudly—and who oversaw everything from the finishing of breadcrusts at breakfast to the smoothing out of a Czerny piano exercise before bedtime. Variety Number Two was equally despotic, but chose to remain uninvolved a good deal of the time, leaving it to his wife to play the "heavy" with the kids, concerning himself not with means but with ends, remaining aloof from the pettier details of day-to-day family life but descending like a ton of concrete if results were less than first-rate.

My father fell into the first category. Correction: My father *invented* the first category. A natural monarch, he was powerful of lung, sharp of tongue. At first his monarchy rested, secure and unchallenged, upon these two God-given attributes as well as upon his skillful employment of two basic tactics that enhanced his power and defeated my plans every time. The first was to manipulate my age to suit his case. One moment he would argue, "You're too young to decide such things. What does a little kid know about life anyway?" If that didn't discourage me, he would immediately switch tack, like a shrewd sailor on a sea of changing winds. "Look at you, almost a man already; it's time you put aside such childish ideas and faced responsibility." My age was thus a relative concept; it depended at any given moment upon who wanted what to be decided which way.

His other tactic was to ask, after I had gingerly announced some controversial plan or another, "Are you crazy, or are you out of your mind?" The question, of course, presented an impossible choice and stumped me every time. I carried on in this state, a boy one minute, a man the next, never completely sure whether I was in or out of my mind, launching youthful schemes and watching them sink in the tidal wave of his personality.

Then, one day, I discovered in a *Reader's Digest* article the theory that insanity and genius often go hand in hand. Comforted by the thought that what my father took for madness on my part was in fact sheer brilliance, I began the slow painful process of ascendancy, discarding with increasing boldness questions of age and lunacy as irrelevant and immaterial. By the time I was twelve we co-existed, father and I; gasoline and fire housed side by side under the same roof, combustion never more than a tiny spark away.

Minor conflicts now were usually resolved after a short sharp clash of tempers by whoever managed to shout loudest and longest. Occasionally, when such confrontations were staged in father's store, the saleswomen would discreetly declare a half-hour holiday and retire to the coffee shop next door until the "All Clear" was signalled.

Conflicts of a medium size—the sort that couldn't be settled on a one-to-one basis—were submitted for arbitration to a neutral third party, usually one of father's neighbouring businessmen: the druggist, the barber, the manager of the liquor store across the street. This particular forum suited my causes best, for almost always I emerged the victor. There is no appeal like that of a tear-stained boy who wants a box camera or a dollar to go to the circus. Besides, it's so easy to be permissive with somebody else's kid. Inevitably the arbitrator, playing the role of nice guy to the hilt, would wink at my father and say, with incredible good nature and understanding, "Aw, let the kid have what he wants."

Once, when I proposed to take apart my brand-new two-wheeler as a shop-mechanics project at school, father—to whom my bicycle was a sacred object—decided not to take any chances with the regular neighbourhood referees; instead he brought the matter before the rabbi for adjudication. As defendant at these proceedings, I chose to rest my case at the very outset, giving the prosecution plenty of leeway to submit evidence that I was too young, too old, just plain crazy, and without a shred of proper respect for the material possessions he bought for me with his hard-earned money. The rabbi weighed the evidence solemnly. He allowed as how a bicycle was very special, probably the most expensive thing you could give a boy (remember: this was twenty years before transistors). Nevertheless it stood to reason that anything constructed of parts was nothing more than the sum of those parts and need not be regarded as an inviolable whole. Two and two made four, not five, when one spoke of machinery. In other words, my shop-mechanics project had his blessing.

Father suffered this latest adverse ruling without grace. "What the hell do rabbis know about bicycles anyway?" he grumbled as we drove away from the clergyman's house.

Faced with a steady string of losses in both the secular and religious courts, my father abandoned the trial system, discharged the druggist, the barber, the liquor store manager, the rabbi. Victory after victory had made me more brazen. It was time for him to climb back into the saddle, to be once again the whole judicial system rolled into a single personage—prosecuting attorney, judge, jury, appeal court, sheriff, and meticulous keeper of criminal records. But this time the badge and the old six-shooter wouldn't do; he would need a new weapon. And a new weapon he found; a weapon that arrived fresh daily by mail all the way from New York City a thousand miles to the east, one that was available in an inexhaustible supply, that discharged its force silently but with deadly effect and disappeared next day innocently wrapped around some household garbage.

That weapon was the Jewish newspaper.

In the major conflict that began to take shape between my father and me—the conflict concerning my future occupation—I learned that if the pen was mightier than the sword, the Jewish newspaper was mightier than a 75 mm. howitzer.

A word here about the importance of the Jewish newspaper, in those days.

To the smalltown Jew, news was not so much a matter of quantity as quality; no newspaper could earn his readership simply by claiming to print all the news that was fit to print; it had to be the right kind of news. And the right kind of news was to be found in one or the other of the two most popular New York Yiddish-language dailies, *The Day* and *Forward*: tales of marital discord, reunions of long-lost relatives, clinical woes, triumphs over poverty and persecution. Stories of filial disloyalty and parental suffering—stories that tore out the reader's heart— were a great favourite. (Every Jewish father in town had played King Lear in real life at one time or another.)

Of course, the front pages were full of Roosevelt and the New Deal, Hitler and the New Tyranny, and the wars in Ethiopia, Spain and China. These events, however, had no immediate impact upon the smalltown Jew. How could one be expected to be profoundly moved by events in Washington or Nanking when one hardly bothered about affairs in

Sudbury, less than two hundred miles distant over the primitive washboard that was Highway 17 in the thirties? Massive political movements, social upheavals—the stuff of history—were happening on some other planet. Meanwhile, here and now, life had to go on. Goods had to be sold. Bills had to be paid. Money had to be put aside—somehow—for a child's education, and for the lonely rainy days of his parent's old age. The Jewish newspaper, even though it was made up and printed in another land, indeed in another world, knew intimately every iota of the strugglesome life of the small-town Jew. Its pages were filled with the earthy humour of the garment trade, with sympathetic advice on just about everything from bunion-trimming to brain surgery; it articulated his fears and frustrations and offered him, if not solutions, at least the comfort of knowing he was not alone in the wilderness; it nurtured his ambitions, not so much for himself as for his children. If he had to be content to exist in a two-by-four world, that was one thing. But his children would have to rise above this. Life offered greater challenges than selling dresses and scrap metal and Florida oranges.

I have gone to some pains to describe the influence of the Jewish newspaper so that you will have some understanding of how, in the aforementioned major conflict that developed in our household, it became my father's staunchest ally and my own most dreaded adversary.

Now to the war itself.

It broke on my thirteenth birthday with the pronunciamento: "My son is going to be a doctor." This was greeted with universal approval; what higher calling could any man possess? "Doctor." The very word conjured up a picture of a young miracle worker strolling benignly among his patients, they reaching out adoringly to touch his white coat or to let his magic stethoscope brush against them, blessing his pale delicate hands, calling out his name in reverential tones reserved for popes and emperors, begging for his attention—"Doctor, please. . ." Think of the title, and the honour. Better still, think of the money!

Only one person failed to approve the idea—me. I had stood by, one summer at the cottage, while one of the older Jewish boys in the community, a medical student, performed an autopsy on a dead frog, observed him struggling to commit to memory a formidable list of Latin body parts, overheard his parents boast of how hard their son worked to justify their financial sacrifices. None of this was for me.

"I'm going to be either a car designer or a writer," I declared.

"A car designer? A writer? Are you crazy, or are you out of your mind?"

As a car designer, father warned, I'd spend the rest of my days in oil-stained overalls, fingernails permanently grease-caked, patching tires and welding fenders like the men at the service station.

And as for writing, that was even less respectable. "Where have I ever needed a writer?" he demanded. "I've been in business all my life, I've never once needed a writer. A doctor, yes, many times. Even two or three times a lawyer—may they all rot in hell, those crooks. But a writer?"

And he was right. He had never needed a writer.

There were no poet laureates, no writers-in-residence in the clothing trade. From time to time if creative writing was called for, the merchant supplied it himself, composing newspaper advertisements and window posters in the standard prose of the industry: "High Quality at Low Prices" . . . "Lease Expired, Everything Must Go" . . . "Once in a Lifetime Opportunity to Stock Up". . . "Selling Out to the Bare Walls". . . and that most charming of all seasonal greetings "Merry Xmas."

Business correspondence was similarly functional, and minimal: a manufacturer's invoice stamped "Account Over-due"; a merchant's response ("Go to hell") scribbled across the face of the invoice and mailed back. All quite terse and to the point.

So who needed a writer?

Besides, there was the matter of lifestyle.

"I knew writers in Russia," he said. "Never made a ruble, any one of 'em. Sat around in the restaurant all day drinking tea and bumming cigarettes, so broke most of the time they lived off whores. Is that the kind of life you want?"

Frankly it wasn't. In my mind I had envisioned a far different life. I had gone twice to see *Foreign Correspondent*, a Hitchcock thriller starring Joel McCrea as an American newspaperman thickly involved in an underground fascist plot in Europe. I was inspired by that movie (and still watch it every time it shows up on late-night television). McCrea embodied everything I pictured for myself: trench coat, snappy fedora, trans-Atlantic flights and phone calls, diplomatic luncheons in palatial dining rooms, editors barking "Hold the press!" as the big news scoop clattered in on the teletype. New places, new faces, briefcase plastered with stickers reading "Amsterdam," "London," and "Paris." On the go all the time. That was for me.

But to my father this lifestyle was pure gypsy. It ran contrary to his whole way of thinking. To one who had grown up drifting from country to country, from town to town, who craved nothing more than a plot of land to call his own and who finally acquired it—a rectangle of earth thirty by a hundred and twenty, not much but fixed and forever immovable—the idea of a son unrooted to desk and diploma, flying constantly to far-off capitals, with no stock-in-trade save a sheaf of notepaper and a portable typewriter, was anathema.

"You were born to be a doctor."

"I wasn't born to be anything," I countered. "I'm going to be a writer!"

So went the initial skirmish. No thundering barrage, no mortal hand-to-hand combat. The process resembled more the opening round of diplomatic talks: a decree sternly handed down, a counter-decree promptly handed back up, followed by a frank exchange of views and a fruitless attempt to agree upon the text of a joint communique.

Preliminaries over, I made preparations to fight the rest of the war along traditional lines. Expecting that whole sections of the local populace would eventually become caught up in this clash, I set to work moulding public opinion in my favour. I was positively genial to the barber, the druggist, the liquor store manager; I displayed a sudden fascination with Hebrew lore much to the rabbi's surprise and delight; I even went out of my way to establish rapport with the rabbi's wife by insisting upon her recipe for noodle pudding—an unusual request considering that I had never before (nor have I since) attempted to cook a noodle pudding. With the possible exception of the town drunk, I courted everybody and anybody likely to contribute his or her two cents worth for my benefit.

Looking back, I would have to admit all this laying on of charm was—in a word—sickening. Still, I needed all the allies I could muster. So what if, in the process, I had stooped to just about every false and ingratiating act imaginable, short of kissing babies? War was war.

I dug in, a one-man Maginot Line, waiting for the blitz. But the big gun on the other side of the boundary was silent. I waited. And waited. January, February and March blew themselves away and became bleak memories. It was April now, and still my adversary held his fire. Trees budded, the first brave robins arrived and sang of spring; from the docks along the waterfront the steamships stretched their long steel hulls, broke free of their icy winter prisons and moved cautiously into the narrow strip of black water at the mid-point in the St. Mary's River channel, their whistles blasting a baritone version of the robin's spring song.

Then, on a calm balmy evening late in May, the first salvo landed suddenly in my territory. It didn't come zinging over, as I had expected; rather it drifted over (if a salvo can ever be said to drift) —casually, like a Sunday stroll, quietly like an early-morning mist.

"Look at that," father said. He held up the Sunday rotogravure section of *Forward*. The expression on his face was that of an explorer who had just stumbled upon the Eighth Wonder. "Just look at that. Isn't that a beautiful sight?"

I looked. It was a page full of graduation portraits. Young faces, fresh-looking despite the unflattering sepia tones of the roto, looked out at the world from under academic caps. All wore ceremonial black gowns and sheepskin collarbands.

"They all look like Mr. Chips to me," I said.

"Mr. Chips my eye. Read. Here, look at this one."

The captions were in both Yiddish and English. I read the latter aloud.

"Mr. and Mrs. Harry Garfinkle of Ocean Parkway, Brooklyn, are proud to announce the graduation of their son, Dr. Marcus Philip Garfinkle from Columbia Medical School. Dr. Garfinkle topped off a brilliant academic record by winning . . ." There followed an impressive inventory of scholarships and medals.

"What's Harry Garfinkle's son got to do with me?" I

asked. "I never even heard of the Garfinkles. Do we know them?"

"Of course we don't know them, Ivan!" (Ivan, pronounced *"Eevun"* in the Russian manner, was the name father would bestow on me when I was especially obtuse; it placed me in the same mental category as those muscular Siberian dunces alongside whom he had served in the Czar's militia.) "Here, read another one."

"Bound for a career in surgery is Dr. Henry Leo Rosenfeld, son of Mr. and Mrs. Samuel Rosenfeld . . . Dr. Rosenfeld's older brother, Milton, is an eminent surgeon in Cleveland . . ."

"Lucky father. Two surgeons he's got. Here, look at this one."

I read again. ". . . Dr. Levine leaves shortly for postgraduate training in England, having earned the J. Peabody Winterbotham Award for excellence in pathology . . ."

"More!"

I read on. One by one I went through the entire page of portraits. Each caption was pure press-agentry and must have been composed by a highly-paid public relations counsel or at least an adoring mother. Not a single one of this spring crop of sawbones was mediocre. Each and every one had graduated magna-cum-everything; each and every one of them was destined to earn a Nobel Prize in medicine before he reached thirty.

"Well?" father said.

I suppose a dramatic reaction was in order at this point. I suppose I ought to have seen the light, ought to have laid down my sword and shield, ought to have fallen into my father's arms—like the prodigal son returning to the paths of righteousness—and cried "I will, I will. Lead me to the medical school. I will make you proud of me. I will be the youngest Phi Beta Kappa west of Suez. I will discover cures for cancer, corns, and the common cold. I will win not one but three Nobel prizes for medicine. I will even get my picture in the Sunday *Forward.*"

"Well?" father repeated. "What do you think of them?"

"I bet they've all got freckles and smell from iodine. Not only that, but most of them have small eyes."

The reference to the smell of iodine reflected one of my pet distastes. The reference to freckles and small eyes reflected two of my father's. If there was anything he disliked in a human, one was freckles, the other was small eyes; the latter, he claimed, were a sign of sneakiness. ("Show me a man or woman with small eyes and I'll show you a person you can't trust.")

Father re-examined the page of pictures. Of course there wasn't a single freckle in sight. And as for the eyes, every physician was the lucky owner of two large dark saucers that spoke of love and devotion and moonlit nights in desert hideaways.

"Ivan!" That was all he had to say for the moment.

Then he fell silent. The topic was exhausted. Or so I believed.

But when the following Sunday's *Forward* arrived, out came the roto section and behold—another page of sepia-tinted medics. Once again it was caption-reading time in our household. Once again the writer assigned to this feature rhapsodized: Dr. Steiner worked his way through medical school by playing the fiddle; Dr. Hyman had the highest I.Q. ever recorded in The Bronx; Dr. Feldman was born in Poland and didn't speak a word of English until he was sixteen; Dr. Nathan was about to make his parents the proudest and happiest humans alive by marrying . . . a doctor! Ecstasy of ecstasies. Two doctors in one family, and a husband-and-wife team at that.

On and on I read, caption after caption, all announcing in the same wide-eyed throb-nostrilled prose that the cream of American-Jewish youth—the most golden of golden boys— had made it.

During the remaining weeks of that May, and well into June, we carried on thus. At last—praise be to God!— toward the end of June America's colleges ran out of Jewish medical graduates. Of course I had caught on to the purpose behind all this quite early in the game. "Ivan" I might be, but I was sharp enough to know when I was being conned. The word "brainwash" had not yet been coined, but the technique itself was as old as the hills.

Having gotten wise to my father's game, why didn't I confront him and ask, "Look here, just who the hell do you think you're kidding with all this crap about doctors?" There are three reasons why I didn't: firstly, that sort of raw communication between parent and child just didn't exist in those days. Secondly—going from the general to the par- ticular—such a question put in such a manner to my father would have caused an explosion that would have laid waste most of Sault Ste. Marie; the fallout would be settling over parts of The Western Hemisphere to this very day.

Thirdly, and most importantly, it dawned on me (and when it did I was tempted to run through the streets of the town shouting "Eureka!") that my enemy was using my ammunition—the written word. After all, what was a news- paper but pages of written words? And who wrote all those words? Why, writers, of course.

There was an enormous irony here, but I would say noth- ing of this to him. The logic of it was too simple and he was not a man to be convinced by anything so self-evident. Better to play this game from now on "the Russian way;"

be devious, even mendacious; pretend to be swept up in the thrust of his advance but all the while quietly construct a tunnel beneath him into which he will collapse at the precise moment he thinks he smells victory. Betray my thoughts at this point and he might concoct some new and more aggressive scheme to coerce me into medical school.

A year went by. Again it was commencement time. Again my father, the self-appointed dean, greeted class after class in the pages of *Forward* while I, the dean's unwilling and treacherous assistant, read aloud names and deeds and promises of medical glory.

The year after, it was the same routine. On the surface I smiled, I marvelled, I expressed admiration and even envy. But underground I was tunnelling. My freedom, my life, depended on that tunnel.

In June of 1943, when I was sixteen, I applied for a job as a cub reporter with the Sault Daily Star and was hired. Elated at being accepted for the position, I broke the news to my father.

At that very instant the earth gave way under him. He managed to claw his way to the surface. But into the tunnel beneath him tumbled the white coat, the magic stethoscope, the piece of paper that said "Doctor" in Latin, the hundreds of graduation pictures. All buried. Buried forever.

As for me, I went on that summer to the happiest days of my young life, scooping Reuters, Associated Press, and the continent's major dailies, on the newsmaking activities of the local Ladies' Aid, the Lions Club, and the Monday morning drunk-and-vagrancy courts.

The Lawyer

He couldn't go home. Couldn't, or wouldn't, or both. It was almost eight o'clock, long after our store had closed for the day, long past his or our normal suppertime. Still he sat in my father's small office at the rear of the store, drinking and talking, talking and drinking. As soon as his glass was empty he simply held it out and, without a word—no please, no thank you—it was promptly half-filled with rye whiskey. I was then dispatched to the washroom in the warehouse to fill the other half with water.

It was the time of the Fall Assizes, and he talked about his case that had begun that morning. His client, a Ukrainian, had knifed a fellow steelworker (Irish) almost fatally. A cold-blooded ruthless attack, no. A crime of passion? Yes. The Irishman had sought to dance with the Ukrainian's wife at a wedding party; the wife had refused, the Irishman called her a bloody half-breed, the rest was buried in conflict and confusion. But would the twelve craggy impassive faces in the jury box understand?

"I'll make 'em understand," the lawyer said, extending his glass for yet another refill.

And he would, for he was the best criminal lawyer in these

115

parts. Everyone knew it. And he knew it. His courtroom prowess was formidable; even the Assize judges—those starched, boiled and blackrobed severities from Toronto—tangled with him gingerly.

"This one's not going to be easy," he said. "You don't get much sympathy for a Ukrainian when you've got a bunch of Scottish farmers on the jury. Besides, his wife really is a half-breed. But they're starting to roll with me now, I can tell."

He described in detail his meticulous preparation weeks in advance of the trial: how he would take advantage of his old foe the local Crown Attorney whose knowlege of the laws of evidence could never be as keen as his own; how he would deliberately antagonize the judge from the very outset of the hearing so the Ukrainian would take on the complexion of the underdog rather than the aggressor. Like a general he plotted his strategy, lining up various objects on my father's desk to represent the elements in the campaign: this rubber stamp was the judge, that marble pen-holder was the jury, the large gum eraser was the crown attorney. Close by the jurybox sat the Ukrainian's wife (a large shiny paperclip) attired in a neat pink suit and a small white hat. Yesterday disaster; today uncertainty; tomorrow, or perhaps the day after tomorrow, triumph.

"When I'm finished," the lawyer said, "that jury will give my Ukrainian the keys to the city."

We were the perfect audience, reacting suitably with shock or admiration ("You don't say. . . . Amazing! . . . There isn't another lawyer in town who could have . . .")

Meanwhile the bottle of rye, full when he entered the office just before six, was now consumed down to its last few ounces, yet he showed little effect. Where did it all go? Perhaps, deep within his huge frame, there was some extraordinary apparatus where the stuff was reconstituted and distributed to various parts of his body in one benign form or another.

True, his speech was becoming a bit thick by this time. He had begun crisply, for that was his style; short sentences, simple direct language, delivered in a voice that was not loud but that managed to convey absolute authority—delivered with his massive head slightly lowered and bent forward as if poised for a strike, his eyes fixed in a permanent narrow aperture that gave him a look of shrewdness and cunning, his nose fine and straight and—viewed in profile—coming to a point at just the right distance between forehead and chin. All the handsome features were still intact, but by this time the words were being groped for, the sentences trailing off or running into each other.

Why, I wondered, didn't he do his drinking elsewhere? Why here, in this small office with the cheap used furniture and the girlie calendars on the walls, reflecting the taste of local hardware and feed-and-seed merchants? Surely there were hotels, or private clubs.

Yet he sat and talked on, putting off and putting off some more the unwelcome moment when the bottle would be drained dry and it would be time to go home.

"It's no good, you know," he said, extending his glass to accept the final draught, "no good at all. Too many cases. Too much pressure. Fighting everybody every minute of the time. Every eye in the place on you, watching every move you make. Got to stay alert, can't daydream even for a second."

He sighed deeply, wearily, threw that great granite head back to catch the last possible drop from his glass, and rose slowly, standing in the middle of the small office like a giant fallen tree that managed miraculously to right itself.

"I'd better give you a ride home in my car," my father said to him, helping him on with his coat.

"Home; yes, better go home. She'll be waiting." His eyes, those two narrow penetrating apertures, were focussed upon some distant unpleasant horizon. We helped him squeeze his bulk into the car, then out of it once we were in his driveway. I carried his hat which had refused to stay on his head.

She was waiting.

She stood in the doorway, broad-hipped, solid, calm, like a foundation stone, saying nothing. The porch light reflected on her silver-rimmed glasses, obscuring the eyes that looked out from behind the lenses, making her appear strangely eyeless. Gripping the wrought-iron railing with one hand, accepting his hat from me with the other, he made his way up three steps and across the porch and through the front door of the house with such sudden momentum that she was obliged at the last split second to step aside to avoid being run into. Neither looked back at me as I stood at the foot of the steps. Instead, she slammed the door shut, but not before I heard her voice—cold as the supper that awaited him, "Where've you been, drinking at that Jew's again?"

It was late afternoon, December 24th. A time when the saleswomen in the store began eyeing the clock on the office wall, counting the minutes until closing time. It had become a tradition over the years for my father to play host at a Christmas party for the staff. The party would commence promptly at six.

"Okay girls, the last nudnik has gone. Close up!"

The girls would hastily draw the shades at the front doors, throw the cotton dust covers over the merchandise that lay exposed on racks and counters, and head eagerly for the office where the desk had been cleared and transformed into a bar. Nothing fancy: the inevitable bottle of rye (in those days the only people who drank scotch were those clubby-looking Englishmen in the magazine advertisements), the inevitable cartons of gingerale, a box or two of pretzels, a tin of peanuts. Often the husbands or boyfriends of the saleswomen would drop in and by nine o'clock several reserve bottles, cartons and tins would have been produced and exhausted, and employer-employee relations would be at the high point for the year, both sides pledging unflagging allegiance to each other in the difficult month of January (post-Christmas sale) and the even more difficult month of February (annual stock-taking) that lay ahead.

That was how Christmas Eve was usually spent in our store. But with closing time mere minutes away, the front door was thrown open and there, in the doorway, stood the lawyer. His face was flushed. The crown of his fedora was pushed in on one side so that the hat sat lopsided on his granite head. His overcoat was unbuttoned and wide open despite the raw cold.

He was obviously drunk this time. Too drunk even to attempt to look sober, too drunk to worry about dignity. He stood in the middle of the store, arms half extended as if he were about to pronounce a benediction upon all who stood gaping at him. This time the giant tree, its boughs stretched limply out at its sides, swayed noticeably.

"Look here," he commanded, "you've gotta help me, see. It's Chrizmuss. I mean tomorrow is . . . an' I hafta get 'er something. Can't go home without presents for the bitch."

The saleswomen exchanged embarrassed glances. One, spotting the hands of the clock at six sharp, muttered "Damn." My father, anxious to keep the ranks happy, came forward nobly. "Girls, you go into the office and start. I'll look after our friend here." He winked at them reassuringly and gestured to them to disappear into the office, which they did without argument.

The lawyer advanced to the counter on which stood the cash register, an old-fashioned piece of machinery that resembled the console of a mighty cathedral organ. He laid his hand over the top and smiled, not warmly but slyly, his narrow eyes retaining their shrewdness even though all other faculties functioned far below their peak.

"I know you Jews," he said. "This thing"—he tapped the cash register with his forefinger—"this plays your favourite music, doesn't it?"

He dug clumsily into his pocket, and his fist emerged and opened, spilling a crumpled pile of bills on the counter. There were tens, twenties, even one fifty-dollar bill—a sight not commonly beheld in those times.

"I got 'im off, y'know."

"Got who off?"

"The fella with the knife. I told you I'd get him off, an' I did, by Christ. I got the bugger off. And this"— he pointed to the bills—"this is the balance of my fee. Well, almost the balance."

The beverage room in the hotel across the street had the spent portion.

"Let's start with a dress for her; somethin' good now, y'hear? I don't want any of your damn monkey business just because I've been drinking. I want something good."

My father's accomplished eyes had counted the bills almost the moment they landed. He moved happily to the most expensive rack of dresses, summoning the lawyer to follow him.

"What size does she take?"

"How th'hell should I know. She's short and—" He indicated that she had considerable girth.

"It would be better if we knew her right size. We do have a store policy that we don't accept returns unless it's our mistake," my father cautioned him in a very courteous tone of voice.

"Don't worry about that," the lawyer responded. "I'm pretty sure she comes up to about my shoulder, and she's kinda big around here and here, y'know."

A dress was chosen, then a tweed winter coat, a chenille bathrobe, a couple of satin nightgowns, several pairs of stockings, and a silk scarf. In between choices my father would dart into the office. "Just another minute or two, girls. Have some more pretzels."

The gifts were wrapped in tissue, boxed, and tied; the account was totalled, and what little was left of the money on the counter was handed back. The cash register rang— sang!—and the biggest single sale of the sellingest day of the year was recorded.

"I sure hope everything fits," father said, helping to arrange the boxes in an awkward stack in the lawyer's arms.

The lawyer's eyes looked intently into my father's.

"Do you? Do you really?"

"Yes."

"Well lemme tell you something, my frien' . . . I don't give a good goddam."

And with that generous remark, the giant tree turned and swayed out of the store and into his own Christmas Eve.

The office party began almost a full hour behind schedule. One of the saleswomen, already irked at the delay in the start of festivities, shrugged as if a cold chill had passed through her.

"God, if my husband handed me a Christmas present in that spirit, I'd throw it in his face."

"I'd take it all back right after Boxing Day," said another.

"Bite your tongues," my father said. "You don't get a cash sale like that every day." He filled the waiting glasses. Beaming, he lifted his own glass in the air.

"Merry Christmas," he said.

When the party was over, and all that was left were ashtrays laden to the brim with cigarette butts, and when that terrible late Christmas Eve silence that every smalltown Jew knows and dreads had settled on us, my father turned to me.

"Funny how the world goes 'round," he said. "An Irishman gets stabbed for calling a Ukrainian's wife a halfbreed. The Ukrainian pays a fortune to an English lawyer to get him off in front of a jury full of Scotchmen. And they all end up making a Jew happy for a few minutes on Christmas Eve."

Up in Smoke

The line between Good and Evil is thin. In fact, it is thinner than thin; it is practically non-existent. Virtue and sin invade each other's territories freely and no sanctuary on this earth—no matter how lofty—affords absolute protection from wicked thoughts and unlawful deeds.

Take the synagogue in our town, for instance. Erected in the mid-forties after years of patient planning and fundraising, the little red brick building on Bruce Street stood as the crowning achievement of the Jewish community. Here at last was a roof to call our own, with a lawn in front and a mezuzeh on the door and a sign declaring that this was the House of Jacob. No more meetings in the Oddfellows Hall and Foresters Hall, no more High Holiday services in dance halls over bowling alleys.

As one of the three trustees appointed by the congregation to supervise the construction, my father was very proud of the edifice. In the years following its consecration he filled just about every post from steward to president. The House of Jacob was the object of some of his noblest efforts.

It was also the site of the one desperate crime he committed in his seventy years.

My father had a weakness for a particular brand of American cigarettes. Blindfolded, put in a room with a hundred different cigarettes all burning at once, he could quickly sniff out and lead you directly to his favourite brand. That make, and that make alone, satisfied his craving. What's more, he was a smoker of Olympic capacity, running through as many as three packs a day with hardly a pause for breath. Such demands for Yankee Tobacco—and lots of it—would have created agonizing frustration in the average Canadian. But my father was lucky; he lived in a border town. A simple ten-minute ferry ride across the St. Mary's River brought him to the land of plenty— Sault Ste. Marie, Michigan—where he would stock up often and generously.

There was one disadvantage: in a small border town the customs officials eventually got to know the steady travellers a little too intimately. No need to post up a "front-and-side" photograph of my father in the customs office; they knew him by heart. It was a reasonable assumption that he wasn't journeying regularly to the U.S. side of the border just for a change of scenery (there was no change of scenery, for that matter). Eventually, it behooved the smuggler to be a little less cavalier, a little more prudent.

My father, therefore, prevailed upon tourist friends from the States to transport the precious contraband into town for him. This they did with such zeal the first summer that by the end of August his closets were crammed with several cartrunk-loads of cigarettes. And still the tourists continued to arrive, the September hay-fever sufferers from Michigan and Illinois and Ohio who sought relief in our clean clear northern air. And with them came still more cigarettes, carton after carton of the stuff.

Then came bad news: the R.C.M.P. announced the beginning of a campaign to stop cigarette smuggling. There

would be closer scrutiny at border points, personal inspec-
tions, cars would be turned inside-out, suspect premises
would be raided and searched, arrests made.

Surveying his cornucopious closets, my father worried out
loud, "Where in hell will I ever find a safe place to hide all
that?"

Suddenly he had his answer. Hell was no place to stash
the cigarettes; indeed hell was the first place the police
would search. Better to conceal them in heaven, or at least
as close to heaven as one could find in these parts.

The cartons—dozens of them—were promptly packed in
innocent-looking boxes. That very night, when it was late
and the streets were dark and deserted, my father loaded
the entire stockpile into his car and transferred it from his
house to the House of Jacob. As a trustee, he possessed a set
of keys to the synagogue and was familiar with every nook
and cranny of the place. He chose the most inconspicuous
location, a gloomy space under the foyer stairs that was
visited only by the holy spirits who inhabited the building
and by no mortals except himself. There, in that lonely
unlit cache, he laid to rest his forbidden cargo.

From time to time, as his needs dictated, he would make
pilgrimages to the synagogue and dip into his reserves. It
was known that he went to the synagogue often, for in our
town a person's comings and goings were impossible to keep
a secret as long as there was a sun in the sky by day and a
moon by night. But everyone assumed that he was motivated
by a mixture of orthodox piety and devotion to his secular
duties. I alone knew the extra-curricular nature of his attendances.

I regard this as being in essence a religious tale. True,
my father's acts could hardly be termed righteous; still one
must admit that by cloistering his secret stock of American

cigarettes in the temple, he demonstrated an unshakable faith in the Divine.

And there is an element of mystery here, too. (After all, aren't all religious tales founded upon equal elements of faith and mystery?) The mystery is this: our Rabbi—may he rest in peace—was also a devotee of American cigarettes. I wonder where he kept his?

Of Life and Love in a '41 DeSoto

The last thing in the world you did, if you were a teenage Jewish boy in the Sault, was to date a teenage Jewish girl.

The reasons were obvious: firstly, teenage Jewish girls were horrible, each and every one of them. They knew you too well because they had grown up with you. Secondly, and worse still, their parents knew you too well. Whenever you called on a Jewish girl her mother would always look you up and down and burst out laughing. "My God," she would exclaim, "I knew you when you were just a little pisher in diapers, and now look at you." And her father would pinch your cheek until you saw stars.

If a Jewish boy took out a Jewish girl more than twice, the fathers of the boy and girl would joke openly about the future relationship of their families and arrange to inspect each other's financial statements and bank books so that the young couple would be guaranteed a proper economic start in life—all of which joking and arranging was positively mortifying to the young couple itself. Occasionally it turned out that the two sets of parents hadn't been on speaking terms for several years; as a result, any proposed union of boy and girl could hardly be expected to receive official

127

blessings at home and was therefore doomed. Indeed, the sins of the parents were always visited upon their children. "Don't go out with her, she's a gold-digger just like her mother. . ." "Stay away from him, he's a stubborn fool just like his father . . ."

If the two Jewish teenagers saw each other quite steadily, rumours that were intended to be amusing would begin to fly throughout the Jewish community, rumours that emanated from Wiseman's Bakery (from whence came most of the important gossip in town). Tales would be told—very hush-hush of course—that the girl's father had found a package of contraceptives belonging to the boy in the driveway of the girl's house. Eventually, the news would reach the ears of the boy's father. When that occurred, the boy's family existed without rye bread and challah for a month or two, or imported their breads from Toronto, until the whole humiliating business blew over and it was once again possible to present oneself at Wiseman's without embarrassment.

There were other reasons for not dating Jewish girls, reasons of a purely scientific nature.

Jewish girls had a propensity for wearing eyeglasses with extra-thick lenses. They were inclined to certain annoying excesses, like overeating and becoming very fat, and using too much Noxzema so that when you danced with them cheek to cheek all you could smell was Noxzema, and you came away with cold cream on your face.

Intellectually, they tended to be terribly aggressive, trying desperately to top every joke you told, and winning higher grades in school in such thoroughly unfeminine pursuits as History, Geography, Physics, Chemistry, English, French, Latin, Mathematics, and even Gym. There was a certain brassiness about Jewish girls. True, they could put on a coy act whenever you tried to feel a chest or rub a thigh in the darkness of the Algoma Theatre. But you knew somehow that when they gathered among themselves—these hard-bitten Jewish wenches—they would describe your inept attempts in clinical detail, punctuating each sentence with shrieks of derisive laughter.

Gentile girls, on the other hand, were totally desirable.

Gentile girls smelled of Evening-in-Paris which they seemed to purchase by the gallon from Woolworth's or Broughton's Drug. Their hair, never worn in tight phony-looking curls like Jewish girls' but allowed to drop naturally to the shoulder, shone like polished walnut or wheat in a sunny field. In the winter they wore loose-fitting sweaters and pleated plaid skirts that gave them a warm, woolly appearance.

Because every Jewish family possessed a good car "for the business," Jewish boys were renowned for being mobile on weekends. Despite wartime gasoline rationing, each Jewish merchant in town had his own secret knack for maintaining a full tank at all times. After all, wasn't a storekeeper just like a doctor? One never knew when one would have to make a sudden delivery. Gentile girls appreciated this fact of war, and demonstrated their appreciation generously. On Saturday night, when the keys to the family DeSoto were ceremoniously handed over to you ("Remember son, cars don't grow on trees, be careful!"), you would call on your Gentile date and you could sense the moment she climbed into the car that she much preferred this method of transportation to the "Y" dance than walking or going by bus. Unlike her Jewish counterparts who merely took such luxury for granted, a Gentile girl sat on the front seat of the DeSoto very close to you and complimented you on your skill at the wheel, while you pretended to reach for the gearshift lever on the floor and shifted her knee instead.

A visit inside a Gentile girl's home was a journey full of fresh experience. No smell of chicken fat or mothballs here; no mezuzeh at the entrance door. Instead, other smells, other religious symbols. If she were Finnish, the place smelled of fresh strong coffee. If she were Ukrainian, you immediately detected a pungent mixture of cabbage and garlic. An English girl's house often bore the lingering odour of grilled bacon, and an Italian's girl's residence was so saturated from cellar to roof with cheese that the smell entered your nostrils even before the front door had been opened to let you in.

Protestant living rooms usually displayed a copy of a church bulletin in the magazine rack. This presented no special problems. But Catholic living rooms almost invariably were dominated by a fair-sized crucifix on the wall, hung dead-centre above the chesterfield. This made cosy chesterfield conventions very difficult indeed. On some crucifixes Christ's eyes were turned heavenward, on others His eyes were cast downward. No matter. The point was: He was there, in the room with you. "Forgive them, Lord," He seemed to be saying, "for they know not what they do." It was quite impossible to sustain a "Two's Company" atmosphere with Jesus Christ suspended a few inches above your head.

So there, briefly, are all the principal reasons why—despite the odd minor inconveniences—a Jewish boy was always better off dating a Gentile girl. All the principal reasons, that is, save for the most basic: Gentile girls happened to be in plentiful supply and came in a limitless variety of shapes, sizes and temperaments, while Jewish girls were always in short supply (a fact of life shrouded in numerology and genetics, I think) and those that were available were, as I indicated at the outset, all horrible anyway.

It was thus perfectly natural that, in his travels from adolescence to manhood, every Jewish boy should engage in at least one heavy love affair with a schiksa—a Gentile girl. And it was equally natural that his parents should react by becoming bundles of electric wires—short-circuited, sparking, sputtering, fraying at their ends, threatening to burn down the house. Through these high-tension wires coursed all sorts of nervous currents.

There were currents of fear: "Just you wait, my boy, the first time you have an argument she'll call you a dirty Jew."

There were currents of resentment: "How could you do this to us? Haven't we given you everything?"

Currents of anger: "Keep this up and so help me God we'll cut you off without a cent to your name."

Above all, currents of shame: "What will people say?"

If your romance with a Gentile girl took on a really serious appearance—something more than attendances at Boat Club dances and nights of mild petting in Bellevue Park—and if there were genuine indications that you were being magnetized toward some alien altar in an Anglican or Presbyterian or Roman Catholic sanctuary, your parents would adopt a different approach. No more simple hollering, for it was too late in the game and you were too old to be intimidated. Instead, they would reason with you, reason by example. They would point to notorious local intermarriages—of which there were a surprising number in Sault Ste. Marie—and underline for you all of the unspeakable tragedies that had flowed from those unholy unions.

"Do you know that his father sat shiva for a whole month, not just for one week, when he discovered that they were married?" . . . "Do you know that to this day her mother hasn't spoken so much as one word to her?" . . . "Have you seen what she gives him to eat Friday nights? Pork and beans, may God strike me dead if I'm lying, pork and beans!" . . . "Look at their kids, not Jewish, not Christian, not anything." . . . "He's ashamed to come into the synagogue with her, with his schiksa."

It accomplished nothing. Love always prevailed over reason—even reason by example. Therefore you went right ahead with your romance, convinced in your own mind that you and your schiksa would together explore and chart whole new territories of understanding for the benefit of unborn generations, there in the front seat of the DeSoto.

Like most Jewish boys and Gentile girls, you and your girl had first met in your early high school days. You came from "downtown" where the shopping district was located, and your home was a block or two from your father's store, or perhaps you lived in an apartment above the store. She was an east-ender. Her home was on the best side of the tracks, where the local lawyers and doctors lived, where the most ornate Christmas decorations appeared every December and disappeared every January, where the girls donned white figure-skates in winter and the boys rowed in sculling teams in the summer.

The first encounter at a Y dance was a disaster. Your mother had taught you to do the foxtrot, holding you decently and modestly at arm's length while the radio played "Sunday, Monday and Always." And you had taught yourself to waltz; well, actually it wasn't really a waltz; you simply fox-trotted in three-quarter time. But nobody had taught you to jitterbug and when the nickelodeon in the Y gymnasium began to blare out "In the Mood", you let go her hand and went limp—and, even before you could slink off to a corner and lean miserably against a set of parallel bars, one of the senior boys from the east end had cut in and was traversing the floor, from end to end, in a crouched, relaxed style that bespoke great expertise and self-confidence.

The trauma instilled by your initial flop on the dance floor lasted for months. You passed the girl in the halls, you stared across at her in the school auditorium, once you even sat next to her in a booth at Capy's Grill, noting that of all the girls in the restaurant she was the only one who poured her ketchup into a neat little circle at one side of her plate of french fries and who ate the golden brown slices of potato one at a time rather than bunched into a red mess on the fork. She alone, among all the loose-fitting sweaters and pleated plaid skirts, finished her Coke without making a rasping sound as her straw drained the last of the liquid and began to suck air.

In short, she had class. Still, you dared not ask her again for a dance.

Meanwhile, she began noticing things about you.

You were now a sergeant in Squadron 155 Air Cadets of Canada and were privileged to march alone on parades at the rear of your flight rather than in the ranks with the corporals and underlings.

Since your parents had always discouraged most forms of athletics, and since you hadn't much natural aptitude for athletics anyway, you didn't go near the water, didn't go near the hockey arena, the football field, the basketball court, the baseball diamond or the ski hill. Instead, you concentrated on the highbrow. You went near the piano keyboard, you went near the school English and oratorical clubs, you went near student politics. You threw yourself into these occupations, bearing in mind what your parents had drummed into you so often: "You have to be twice as good as they are before they consider you half as good." "They" referred to east-end Gentile society, of course.

By the time you had reached your second-last year of high

school you had won several piano awards at the Kiwanis Music Festival and played in the school orchestra. You had placed second in the oratorical contest and had been elected to your third term on the Students' Council.

In short, while you didn't exactly have class, you were a Somebody.

You still hadn't mastered the jitterbug but it didn't matter anymore; as one reached one's senior years in high school it was the slow numbers that counted, especially the final number on the dance program—"Goodnight, Sweetheart"—when the girls danced with their eyes closed and the boys buried their faces in the girls' hair and the floor seemed to be coated with sweet sticky corn syrup that made you take small intimate steps.

So, putting aside those ghastly memories of earlier times, you caught her outside the chemistry lab one Friday afternoon at four o'clock and invited her to celebrate the end of yet another drab week of school over a Coke at Capy's Grill, an invitation she accepted with unexpected enthusiasm.

After that the invitations and the acceptances grew in number and importance. You continued to look at the other Gentile girls who shared your teenage world, but you didn't really see them. She, meanwhile, had begun turning down invitations from one of the basketball stars who was constantly after her, and brushed off the son of one of the higher-up executives at the steel plant, a young man with great expectations—his father having been to Yale. Several of the boys who left high school to go into the services, and who returned home for short leaves looking smart in their crisply-creased uniforms, called her for dates. One of the boys even had his wings and was reputed to have topped his class at the flying school at Camp Borden. Still she said no, she was busy.

At last you were both in the final year of high school and going steady. There were no official announcements. One simply concluded that the same boy and the same girl, seen together regularly in a booth at Capy's, or dancing by themselves in a dark corner of the gym at the Y Saturday night after Saturday night, or joined together on the front seat of a DeSoto on Sunday afternoons, were irrevocably committed to each other. Among your peers that is what one simply concluded.

With your parents there was the same conclusion, to be sure. But it was not a simple conclusion, arrived at calmly and with resignation. Far from it.

"Where are you going, out with that same schiksa tonight? Do you know, do you have even the *slightest* idea, just what the hell you're getting yourself into? Have you made up your mind to throw away everything just for this girl?"

To all of these questions the answer was yes. Yes, you were going out again with her because there wasn't a Jewish girl anywhere in the Western Hemisphere who possessed even the tiniest fraction of this girl's softness and gentleness. Yes, you knew exactly what the hell you were getting into. You'd been in her home many times now and not only were her parents kind to you but there wasn't even a crucifix on their living room wall (it hung in the entrance hall near the coatrack), and they had never so much as breathed a word in your presence about the fact that they were Catholics and you were Jewish. Yes, if necessary you were prepared to throw away everything for this girl; a chance to get out of the small town, a chance to go to college, a chance to carve out a career for yourself in some big city hospital or courtroom. If necessary, you were prepared to spend the rest of your days with her, there in the front seat of the DeSoto, parked on the Canada Steamships dock at the foot of Pim Street, watching the lake freighters go by on the St. Mary's River, surviving on Cokes, french fries, and dreams.

Then, late one Saturday night after the dance at the Y was over, you'd consumed the traditional hot roast-beef sandwiches with french fries and peas all drowned in thick brown gravy, had parted company with the other kids in your clique, and had parked on one of the few unoccupied promontories that could still be found at that hour in Bellevue Park.

She sat very still, her eyes looking straight ahead through the windshield at the dark river.

"I don't know how to tell you this," she said quietly, "but my mother and father had a long talk with me last night ..."

It was all over just as it had begun years before at that first dance—painfully.

At home you were once again persona grata. The war was coming to a close and, with victory in sight and the cash registers cheerfully ringing, your father spoke of buying you one of the first new cars that would soon come off the assembly lines and of outfitting you for university with your first made-to-measure overcoat. Your mother stopped nagging you about everything. You could deposit your dirty laundry right smack in the middle of the dining room table and she would kiss your socks, so happy was she to have her son back in the fold again where he belonged.

In the autumn following the Big Breakup, the girl entered the rigorous and disciplined life of a nurse-in-training at the local Catholic hospital. You went off to college in Toronto where you were accepted into a fashionable Jewish fraternity. There, in the fraternity house, you learned the first social lesson for living in the big city: "Jewish girls are 'nice' girls; them you take out when you want to spend a respectable evening and you've got some money to spend. Schiksas are the ones you take out when you have 'other things' in mind."

One day, early in your freshman year, you spoke to a girl who always seemed to sit near you during English classes. You told her your name and she said hers was Gretta Brockman.

Gretta Brockman. Jewish! And a doll at that. Flawless complexion. A great way of walking. And twenty-twenty vision.

"I've got tickets for the play at Hart House Saturday night," you said. "How'd you like to join me? Maybe we could have a bite first . . ."

You took her to dinner at the Savarin where she ordered filet mignon and strawberry shortcake, the latter out of season and very expensive. You told her where you were from and a bit of your past history. Then you asked her about herself.

"Gretta Brockman," you said, lying, "that name's awfully familiar. Where would I have heard your family's name before?"

She paused to think, anchoring her fork in the strawberry shortcake. "Gee, I don't know where you would have run across it. We're the only Brockmans in Toronto, as far as I know. I've never heard my folks speak about any relatives up north."

She then explained that her real name was Gretchen Braukmann, that her father was born in Germany and her mother in Denmark. "We live in York Mills, quite close to a Lutheran church—which is handy because we're Lutherans."

Down the drain went your filet mignon and your shortcake, down the drain went your theatre tickets. Down the drain. Wasted.

You'd come a long way from Sault Ste. Marie.

But you still had a long way to go.

The Making of the President, 1944

In the summer of 1944 Thomas E. Dewey, New York's Republican governor, embarked upon the impossible task of replacing Franklin D. Roosevelt as president of the United States of America. It was an historic battle: Dewey, the sober young ex-district attorney attacking the gates of the White House demanding to be let in; Roosevelt, resolute despite his age, infirmity and war-weariness, insisting upon remaining in occupancy for an unprecedented fourth term. One man desperately seeking the highest office in the land, the other just as desperately refusing to give it up.

In that same hot July of 1944 our Jewish community was engaged in the annual agony of hunting for a president. But in this case it may truly be said that the man did not seek the office, the office sought the man. Mind you, this was not a new state of affairs. Traditionally, a president was pressed into service in a manner very much resembling the recruitment of seamen into the British Navy in days of yore. In fact, the only difference lay in the technique of bludgeoning; where a potential sailor was persuaded with a wooden club, a potential president was persuaded with wild promises and even wilder threats. In either case, by the time the victim recovered consciousness, he was far out to sea and committed to a year of misery. Only in the rarest instances did a draftee for the presidency accept the call without putting up strong resistance. Such a man usually possessed a streak of vanity a yard wide. But by term's end vanity had changed to thorough disenchantment; consequently there was never a problem over an incumbent succeeding himself—the incumbent couldn't wait to abandon his gavel.

Putting aside all false notions of nobility, the truth is that leading a smalltown Jewish community was a thankless enterprise. A leader could rarely delegate authority simply because his peers were seldom—if ever—in a mood to take orders. If, however, the leader took matters into his own hands, he was forthwith accused of being autocratic and shunned anyway. The budget made generous allowances for nothing, and what little finances were available to support the rabbi-teacher-shoichet, the Sunday school, and the odd small capital purchase, depended upon the largess of two or three affluent members who had to be catered to as a rich old dowager is catered to in a hotel dining room. Decorum at meetings hung always in a precarious balance between anarchy on one hand and mass sleeping sickness on the other. A call to order at the beginning of a meeting was as futile a gesture as trying to halt a cattle stampede with a capgun. Motions to adjourn came with lightning surprise, entirely without invitation or welcome from the chair, and most of the congregants were in their cars and halfway home by the time the motion was seconded by one of the president's less disloyal constituents.

With little hope of co-operation, no pay, and nothing to look forward to but an empty vote of gratitude when the term of office expired, was it any wonder that an intelligent man fled in terror when his fellows attempted to cast the presidential mantle upon his shoulders?

But now, in 1944, there was a fresh occupational hazard that made filling the post even more difficult. The war, the stories of Nazi oppression of Jews, and entry into the armed forces of a dozen local Jewish young men—all these events had made our congregation the object of considerable curiosity and sympathy. Thus it was that by 1944 the usual criteria for judging presidential material had to be expanded to include one new and important requirement: the incoming president would have to know how to handle himself among "the goyim."

Fully aware of this new turn of events, the "press gang," a quartet of self-appointed kingmakers in the Jewish community, gathered to pore over the list of potential chief executives. Their headquarters was the workroom at the rear of Wiseman's Bakery on Queen Street. Save that the room was filled with the aroma of freshly-baked bread rather than cigar smoke, it resembled any back room where major political decisions are made. A swinging door with a tiny peek-through window separated the workroom from the public premises at the front. On the door was tacked a handwritten sign: Private Keep Out!

In the days before the Gin Rummy Club rented luxurious quarters (one room about fifteen by twelve with adjoining toilet) over Kleiman's Hardware, the closest thing in town to a Jewish men's club was Wiseman's Bakery. To this place the men would escape in the evenings, having assured their wives they would only be gone long enough to buy a fresh loaf for tomorrow's breakfast. Here too they discussed important questions of the day: how come the town's most aggressive merchant managed to stage *three* anniversary sales within a single year? Was there some brand new element of time in the universe known only to him? And how come the town's least lucky merchant was running another going-out-of-business sale? How many times in a single year, in a single store, could a man go out of business? Whose son was sleeping regularly with a "Talyainichka" from the west end? And was it any big surprise, considering the son's father had been residing off and on with a "Polyachka" for years?

These musings were presided over by Wiseman himself. Bearing the physique of a grizzled old drayman, Wiseman flopped about flat-footedly in his oversize flour-covered shoes, one minute gruffly attending a customer out front, the next minute bear-hugging a hundred-pound sack of flour and transporting it from one end of the workroom to the other, moments later returning to the long worktable laden with small mounds of dough waiting obediently in neat rows to be shovelled into the hearth by their master.

The men, seated at the worktable, were impatient. The July heat and the heat from Wiseman's hearth were almost too much, even when urgent affairs of state were on the agenda.

"Come on, Wiseman, put all this chazerai in the oven and let's get down to business."

Having fed his ovens, Wiseman sat down on a high stool, his broad wrestler's hands resting squarely on his baggy knees. The House was now officially in session.

"So who's it going to be?" he began.

The first order of business—as it had been for years—was for the members of the press gang to disqualify themselves from the running. Of one mind when it came to the perils of electioneering, they agreed that they would be far more content to carry on as the powers behind the power. Not for them the big armchair, the head table, and the gavel. Better to sit in the shadowy background and watch "their man" perform, dosing him with flattery when his morale lagged, and lacerating him with scorn when he dared depart from their advice.

Once again they reviewed the list of desirable qualities. "It's got to be somebody who loves punishment . . . or somebody who's crazy for a little honour and publicity . . . or somebody who's a complete fool . . . or somebody who's got lots of time and nothing better to do . . ."

"Plus"—Wiseman pointed an index finger skyward for emphasis—"plus he's got to be presentable when he goes among goyim."

The others agreed. That was the main requirement now. They needed a candidate who was reasonably fluent in English and who "looked good" too.

"Maybe we should hire Rockefeller if it's gotta be such a fancy duke," one man suggested.

"We don't need a Rockefeller," Wiseman replied. "You'll see, we'll go through the list, we'll find some damn fool who fills the bill." Wiseman beckoned imperiously to the committee secretary. "Read the list and we'll decide one by one."

The reading of the list began in alphabetical order.

"Altman."

"Altman's out. His health won't stand it."

"What do you mean his health won't stand it? We're not asking him to fight Joe Louis."

"He gets colds too easy. He wouldn't last past November eleventh. Don't you remember last year they invited the president to lay a wreath on Armistice Day at the cenotaph in front of the courthouse? The poor sonofabitch froze his tuchis off and was sick in bed for two weeks afterwards. No, Altman's condition isn't up to it, I tell you."

"Berger is next."

"Berger's out too. He's just too goddam smart, and you can't trust a smart guy. Besides, he uses a lot of fancy English words which he doesn't even know the meaning. A real show-off."

"Cramer?"

"Cramer you can forget about," one of the committee said. "He's got his hands full now, that's for sure." The men nodded sympathetically. Cramer did indeed have his hands full, having been charged with numerous violations of the law by an implacable inspector from the Wartime Prices Control Board.

Dorff was out of the question. He had his hands full with his wife and mother-in-law 'watching his every move. "They even follow him to the toilet," one of the committee said, "to see if he's hiding money there."

"Einhorn?"

Ineligible. Einhorn had served one term in the presidency several years ago and hadn't spoken to half the men in the congregation since.

So it went, on down the list, greatness still waiting to be thrust upon some one unsuspecting member of the Jewish community.

At last the committee came to R for Rosen.

"Rosen! Ah, here . . . here is a possibility," one of the men piped up. "Think about it. He's vain like a peacock . . . do you know he's the only storekeeper in town who parades around in the summer in white shoes?"

"And you know something else," another volunteered, "he's the only one that when he goes to Toronto on a buying trip he carries a briefcase around with him on Spadina Avenue."

"A briefcase! You're lying—"

"So help me God it's the truth may my children never have a good day if I'm lying. One of the coat manufacturers told me, and I believe him."

A briefcase: field marshals had their batons, bishops their mitres, lord mayors their chains of office. But a merchant carrying a briefcase as he made his rounds in Toronto's garment district—that had to be the last word in symbols of pomp and grandeur. Not for Rosen suitpockets stuffed with memos and invoices. Rosen had a briefcase, with his initials embossed in gold below the handle and cardboard files inside all arranged in order. Such vanity was unheard of.

"Didn't I tell you he's a peacock?" said the first critic.

"The man loves attention, no doubt about it," said the second.

"He must be a fool if he can't carry his business affairs in his head," said the third.

"A briefcase yet," said the fourth. "Have you ever heard of anything so goyish?"

With this last remark, the presidential nail had been hit on the head. The committee realized they had their man.

The following night the press gang invited Rosen to Wiseman's Bakery ostensibly for an innocent game of poker. The approach was subtle—a couple of hours of card-playing, tea, spongecake, bits and pieces of local gossip. Eventually one of the players brought up the U.S. presidential race.

"That fella Dewey, he's gotta be some schvantz. Imagine taking on a giant of a man like Roosevelt. Only a hundred percent meshuganer would do such a thing!"

Wiseman, alert to this opening signal, immediately carried the play forward. "And for what? For a little power? A little honour? Who needs it. Life's too short."

"Oh, I don't know," Rosen said quietly, leaning back in his chair, his eyes fixed on some distant invisible horizon. He was deep in his own thoughts, no doubt speculating on how he would conduct his campaign if he were Thomas E. Dewey. "A man always has to reach longer than his arms. Otherwise nothing gets accomplished in this world," he said.

There was a quick exchange of glances among the members of the press gang. Rosen was clearly available. But one never pulls suddenly on the line when one has hooked a big fish. One has to "play" the line, now letting out a little, now pulling in a little; then, when all instincts are precisely right, there occurs a split second of unity when captor and captive fuse and become as one. That split second was at hand.

"I don't agree with you, Rosen," Wiseman said, making certain at the same time to refill Rosen's glass with hot tea. "A man's got to know his limits. Some of us are meant to be presidents, and some of us just aren't. That's all there is to it."

"Ach, that's old-country talk," Rosen said, plunking four pieces of lumpsugar into the steaming tea. "In Russia, in Poland, they always told you that you had to know your place. You were born a tailor? Then stay a tailor. Born a butcher? Stay a butcher. In America it's different. Why shouldn't Dewey be the president? Is Roosevelt God or something that he's always got to be Number One? Suppose they had told Abraham Lincoln he shouldn't bother running because he was born in such a lousy log cabin that I wouldn't even park my car there, wouldn't that have been a tragedy?"

"But Lincoln," protested one of the committee, "was no ordinary man, you know. This man was pretty special. A really self-made man."

"We're all self-made men," Rosen interjected. "Tell me, did anybody hand you your businesses on a silver platter?" The men nodded thoughtfully; Rosen had a point.

"But Lincoln had a lot of talent," one of the men countered. "What gift of the gab. Did you ever read any of his speeches and his sayings? A golden tongue, that's what the man was blessed with."

Rosen was unimpressed. "Golden schmolden. You talk long enough in public you get used to being a big talker. All it takes is nerve and practice. A genius you don't have to be. Look at Mackenzie King. There was a time you wouldn't go from one end of this room to the other to hear the man talk. But today he's Prime Minister already a few years so everybody hangs on his words. Everybody says my goodness that man has a way of putting things. And look at the other King, the one in England. A stutterer, poor man. But when he's got to talk, he talks, and pretty good too. Did you hear him last Christmas? It's nerve, that's all."

"So how many of us have that kind of nerve?" Wiseman asked.

"We all have," Rosen replied. "Didn't we come to this country not knowing a single word of English. I went to a cheder in Poland; you think they taught me English there? No sir, I had nerve when I came here and today I can talk to people—to goyim—like I was born here, and they don't even know the difference. I was just saying to Reverend Ferguson's wife yesterday—"

"Reverend Ferguson's wife?" one of the men broke in. "She shops in your store?"

"Sure, what do you think, she shops only in goyishe stores? She comes in, I give her twenty off automatically. I'd like to see her get a discount at Eaton's. Bupkes Eaton's'll give her off."

"He comes in too?"

"The Reverend? Sure, lots of times. We even have some very interesting conversations. He's really a fine goy."

Unwittingly the fish had placed himself in the category
of a catch. Wiseman prepared to net him.

"You know something, Rosen," the baker said, offering
more spongecake, "you're a lucky fella. In fact it's more than
luck; you're a smart fella. Believe me, I'd like to have customers like the Fergusons they should buy from me."

Rosen, a little smug now, shook his head reprovingly.
"People like the Fergusons don't buy rye bread and pumper-
nickel," he scoffed. "You have to know how to deal with
their kind. They're not Polyacken or Talyainer, you know.
With goyim like the Fergusons you talk first about the
weather, about the news. You got to pretend you don't even
give a damn if they buy or they don't buy because it's such
a pleasure to have their company. Then, when they're good
and ready, they tell you what they're looking for."

"You sure know how to deal with those people," Wiseman
said.

"It's not just a matter of dealing any more," Rosen said,
smugness having expanded into pride. "I've been Ferguson's
guest already at the Rotary Club."

These were the magic words the committee had been
waiting for. Of all the service clubs in town, the Rotary Club
was the most prestigious. Eagerly the men questioned Rosen.
Whom had he been seated with? Was his bank manager
there? What did they serve for lunch and was he able to eat
it? Who was the guest speaker? All these queries Rosen
answered in great detail, relishing the special status he now
occupied in his listeners' eyes. One of the men asked, "Did
they say grace before they ate, like you see in the movies?"

Rosen beamed. "Did they say grace? You should hear the
grace they said. It was such a grace, believe me every Jew
in this town should only have such a grace before he sits
down to eat. I only wish my wife and kids could have been

there. They called naturally on the Reverend to say grace. Well, let me tell you, that man made a speech, there were tears in my eyes. He said they should thank God they not only had a good lunch coming but that—and listen to this— but that God was allowing them to share it with one of their distinguished—so help me God he said distinguished—Jewish neighbours. And you know what else—such a fine goy—he didn't use the name of Jesus once, not once! That's what I call a mensch."

Were there incongruities here? Subtleties not easily discerned? Lapses of logic? Unexplained differences and unbridgeable gaps? Perhaps, but it didn't matter. By all outward signs and superficial standards, Rosen was the perfect man for the job, a man whose time had come.

Looking Rosen directly in the eye with an earnestness he reserved for moments when he was being truly insincere, Wiseman, his voice quavering, spoke. "Rosen," he said, "you know it'll soon be time for us to elect a new president." There was a sense of history in the atmosphere. All eyes were on Rosen. "We've decided that the best man for the job . . . is you."

There was dead silence, so much so that the sound of the crusts browning in the hearth could be heard. Rosen looked at the men around him, one by one. "You're out of your goddam minds," he said at last. "You're crazy in the head if you think I would take on such a lousy job. Better I should commit suicide. Show me a man, show me one single man, who hasn't had anything but the greatest aggravation from being president. Look at Einhorn; to this day he doesn't talk to half the people in this congregation and it's already five six years since he was president."

Why argue? Rosen was absolutely right. So the press gang remained silent, permitting their catch to thrash about and convulse in the net. He would soon give one last heave, one last massive gasp, and lie still in total submission to the public will. Meanwhile they listened politely as Rosen reviewed the record of the past dozen presidencies. Each and every leader had left behind a trail of bitterness and discontent. "No thank you," Rosen concluded, "like I said before, suicide would be better."

One of the committee made as if to counter with a point, but Wiseman quickly raised a hand to command silence.

"You should see how the goyim run things at their clubs," Rosen went on. "You should just see the way they got everything organized with committees and reports and rules and regulations just like in Parliament. If I was president, believe me, things would be run the way *they* run them, not the way we run them."

"If I was president . . ." More magic words. Rosen was beginning to visualize himself in office. That was good. Without any urging, Rosen continued to spell out his reform program. "I would see that there was proper respect, and proper order. No more cross-talk and back-talk. No more jumping up in the middle of a meeting and saying to hell with it I move it's time to go home. And everybody on the executive would have to be called by their proper titles: Mr. President, Mr. Secretary, Mr. Treasurer."

The committee, including Wiseman, began to look just the slightest bit uneasy. Rosen, unaware of this reaction, warmed increasingly to his vision of the new order. "I would even have the rabbi give an opening benediction, like they do with their minister."

An opening benediction? The men looked at each other in disbelief. One asked hesitantly, "In what language?"

"In English, of course. You want dignity, don't you?"

No one responded. What, after all, did they want? Dignity? Decorum? Please Mr. Chairman, thank you Mr. Chairman, briefcases, filing systems? These were men who carried their own business affairs filed in the channels of their brains and on the backs of used envelopes. These were men who knew each other as Itzik and Yoshka and Yamkeh and more often by unflattering nicknames—The Weasel, Chooligan, Der Roiter, Grosser Verdiener. Were they now to be transformed into mock-Christians? And in the space of a single year under Rosen's administration? True, this was 1944, not 1934 or 1924; the younger generation, Canadian-born, English-oriented, would soon be moving in to take over community activities. The men couldn't go on forever doing things old-country style. Or could they?

The men of the press gang sat staring at nothing. Someone coughed, a chair scraped against the floor, a spoon rattled inside an empty tea glass.

Finally, Wiseman rose from his stool. "I better see how my bread is doing," he said wearily, shuffling to the ovens.

"Let's play another coupla hands," one of the men said, and he slammed the deck of cards decisively down at the centre of the table.

"Not me," Rosen said, leaving his chair and putting on his jacket. "I gotta go home. My wife'll kill me."

The other men watched Rosen depart. They said nothing until they heard the front door of the shop close behind him.

"You know," said one, "we had him right in the net, hooked and all."

"Sometimes," Wiseman said, "you think you've landed something good, and then you look at the end of the line and it's a lousy catfish. And who the hell eats catfish?"

The old baker turned to the man with the alphabetical list of prospects.

"What comes after R?"

The House on the Rock

"Should we build a synagogue or should we not?"

The proponents of the plan—a handful of shrewd old-timers—sensed that there would be strong pockets of resistance centring around the crucial issue of funds. Though the time was early 1942, the bad breath of the Depression still lingered in the town, and the average Jewish storekeeper hesitated to answer the knock on his door at night for fear he would see a wolf standing there. True enough, a growing wartime economy brought with it the beginnings of prosperity, but the small merchant, accustomed to the hand-to-mouth existence of the thirties, could not be expected to shake off almost overnight the habits of a decade of anxieties. Those who favoured the building of a synagogue therefore took it upon themselves to inspire a little confidence by laying on a banquet which every Jewish man, woman and child in the community was pressed into attending. Delicatessen was imported for the occasion from Toronto, arriving packed with dry ice in large cardboard cartons which—though tightly sealed—yielded such a strong aroma that the train bearing them was that day named "The Garlic Special" by the committee assigned to transport the cargo from the

152

station to the Foresters Hall.

The crowd, rubbing their hands hungrily after trudging through the cold winter night to the Hall, sat at long tables decked with white bed sheets. In the centre of the tables, like sentries posted along a boundary-line, stood bottles of schnapps waiting stiffly at attention to be called up for service. At the signal to begin, there followed a frenzy of platter-passing, bottle-pouring, glass-spilling and mustard-spattering that ended a half-hour later with empty plates and sighs of satisfaction. Seated at the head table, the organizers looked about and saw that all was going well. The time to strike was now when even those who were most difficult to convince would be settling back in their chairs in a state of semi-euphoria, watching the smoke from their cigarettes ascend to the ceiling of the Foresters Hall.

"Ladies and gentlemen, boys and girls, may I have your attention, please . . ." The speaker, who had risen at the centre of the head table, stood waiting for silence, his hands deep in his trousers pockets—his characteristic stance whenever addressing a public gathering. If any other man in the Jewish community rose to speak in this fashion, people snickered, "You see, he's guarding his balls." But when this man —whose nickname was "Der Reicher" (The Rich One)— rose to speak, hands in pockets, people whispered almost reverently, "You see, he's guarding his cash." It wasn't often that Der Reicher undertook to champion social causes. Indeed, he was usually notable for his absences from community meetings, so totally occupied was he with his own business affairs. The man's entrepreneurship was almost limitless: he owned the largest clothing store in town, knew every Indian fur trapper from the Soo to James Bay, memorized the bid and ask for every stock listed on the Toronto market, and could read a profit-and-loss statement faster than most men could read a headline in *Der Tag*. He had even been to Florida once or twice. And now, here he was, not only present in body, but the keynote speaker. Like fire licking its way through underbrush, word was passed down along the tables. "Shah!"

Never a person noted for wasting time on niceties, Der Reicher plunged quickly and directly into the tenderest part of every adult heart. "It is not so much for us as for the children . . ." There was scarcely a man or woman in the audience who hadn't cut off his or her right arm "for the children." Fathers had mortgaged businesses and mothers had pawned wedding rings to put their sons and daughters through college. Winter and summer, debt had hung on their shoulders like a heavy mantle—all "for the children."

The combination of persuasive forces—the smoked meat, the schnapps, Der Reicher diverting his attention from his warehouses and his coffers for a whole evening, and the appeal itself—"It is not so much for us as for the children"—repeated again and again throughout the opening speech was enough to overwhelm the stubbornest opponents. The applause when he sat down told Der Reicher and his fellow-occupants of the head table that they had succeeded. There would be a synagogue in Sault Ste. Marie.

So thoroughly had the organizers done their homework that a slate of three trustees (all of whom had agreed in advance to serve) was quickly accepted by the general body without even a hint of contest from the floor.

The oldest of the three, Mr. Crandel, was well beyond three score and ten years. Every morning as he stared at himself shaving in the mirror, he saw the face of death staring back at him, its eyes heavy-lidded and colourless above the layers of white lather. And he did not like what he saw, for although he was old, and was the proprietor of several flourishing businesses in the town, his work on earth was far from accomplished and he was not yet ready to close his eyes forever. A number of his sons and daughters had married Gentiles and wandered vast distances from his world, and though they had brought no shame upon him or upon themselves, he felt in his heart that he had somehow sinned in allowing this to happen, and that only by performing one last great deed could he atone. He prayed, therefore, each morning as he saw himself in the mirror, that the colourless eyes would remain open another day, another month, another year, so that he could build the synagogue. Before long he thought about the task almost every moment each day: at his meals, at his work, as he lay in bed at night probing the dark sheets for a comfortable place to lay his bones, bones that were once young and powerful and now were old and restless. It became his reason to live. Long a strong advocate for the building of a synagogue, Crandel came to be regarded in the Jewish community as a holy man. And since he knew that he was so regarded, he doubled and redoubled his zeal to see the project come to life. Nobody and nothing would stand in the way of his determination.

The second of the three, Mr. Dreyfus, was about fifteen years younger than Crandel. Being inclined to revere men who possessed many years and much wealth, Dreyfus looked up to Crandel who was both older and richer than he. Unlike Crandel, who felt that he had much to atone for, Dreyfus felt that his books of account in heaven were quite neatly balanced. In all things he did good for others. He took pleasure in providing comforts for his wife and sons, and gave them love which they returned amply. He was respectful to his elders and affectionate toward the young. He was an attentive host, a giver to charity, and dealt justly with his creditors and his customers. When he looked at himself in the mirror, he saw a picture of a life well lived. But he was driven by a constant anxiety to have everyone recognize and appreciate his goodness. And so, whenever a position of honour became available, he seized the opportunity because even the best of men crave and indeed thrive upon public approval. This need for approval led him to be a fence-sitter. Whenever controversy arose—as so often it did—one could not always be sure what stand, if any, Dreyfus would take until the adversaries had exhausted both their arguments and themselves. In fairness, however, it must be said that this trait made him particularly useful; whenever factions seemed hopelessly polarized, Dreyfus was able to play the role of an intermediary and peacemaker. This talent, too, nourished his image as a good man and a man of eternal goodwill. Thus, because Dreyfus was a good man, he maintained neutrality throughout most issues. And because he maintained neutrality, he was considered a good man by everyone.

By everyone, that is, except my father, who was the third and youngest member of the building committee. My father was a fiery flagwaver, the flag of course bearing his favourite colours—black and white; gray was one colour that was seldom painted on his standards. He demanded total loyalty to himself and to any cause he espoused, and anything less than total loyalty he considered treason. Equipped with an intuition that neither slept nor slumbered but functioned overtime, he would size up any matter quickly, form an opinion based on his initial impressions, and adhere to that opinion unswervingly from beginning to end. Uncomfortable in his role as the junior member of the triumvirate, he resented the deference with which Crandel was treated by the congregation, and regarded Dreyfus with a certain wariness. Since my father had some experience in building, and was renowned for "looking after things"—particularly property— he was regarded by the congregation as eminently suited to be one of the overseers of the synagogue project. He could out-bargain and out-shout the toughest carpenter, plumber or electrician in town. Since he could carry off scenes with tradesmen with such authority, he was regarded by others as well as by himself as an expert on all matters of construction and maintenance. This made him out-bargain and out-shout the carpenters and plumbers and electricians all the more. By this point in time, he was quite convinced that, given the challenge of erecting the Empire State Building, he could have the job done from start to finish in six days, leaving the seventh day free to rest, catch up on the week's news in his Jewish papers, and smoke three packages of cigarettes.

Standing now beside Der Reicher, the newly-appointed trustees acknowledged the assembly's applause and shook hands among themselves, Crandel on one side, my father on the other, Dreyfus between them, like two wrestlers and a referee making ready to enter the ring.

Der Reicher spoke again, "Gentlemen, our hearts are with you. May all your many efforts in the future be crowned with success and may God go with you."

But God did not go with them. Instead, He chose at that precise moment to quit the Foresters Hall and go on a very long vacation. Presumably He slipped through an open transom concealed in a cloud of cigarette smoke. For God knew something that the people of the congregation—even the wisest of them—did not know: whenever three men, moved by a noble vision, form a committee to lay a brick, they inevitably mislay the noble vision before the mortar has hardened.

From the very outset there were conflicts.

There was sharp conflict over the choice of the site. One trustee said it should be in the east end of town to reflect the gradual movement by the Jews to the more desirable residential areas there. The other, representing the conservatives, charged that this was an attempt to appease The Four Hundred—a clique who considered themselves rather chic and sophisticated and were having less and less social intercourse with the old-country types. The former retorted that this was nonsense and that locating the synagogue in the east end of town was simply good taste. The latter contended that the deciding factor should be convenience and not taste; therefore, the site should be as central as possible to the Jewish places of business downtown. This way, a shopkeeper could commune with his customers right up until the six o'clock closing time, and be in his pew communing with God by 6:15, all without raising so much as a bead of sweat on his brow. And when it came right down to that, the latter pointed out, were not the two forms of business— God's and man's—so inextricably bound together that one could not flourish except in close proximity to the other? If Dreyfus favoured one part of town over the other, he chose not to reveal his preference and since the issue remained in deadlock it was laid before the general body for a decision. The conservative position prevailed. Land was selected on the west side of Bruce Street, a plot without so much as a square foot of natural charm, situated next door to a welding shop and two addresses removed from a gas station. Looking eastward from this site, one saw not Jerusalem but a dingy confectionery store across the street, its front stoop littered with discarded gum wrappers and Popsicle sticks. On the other hand, it was convenient. Queen Street— the street of daily bread—was only a block away. It was a victory for practicality, and a defeat for aesthetics. The small-scale renaissance that could have taken wing instead plummetted to the earth, landing like a stricken bird right there on the west side of Bruce Street, next to the welding shop and across the street from the confectionery.

There was conflict next over the design concept of the building. "It should have a flat roof with the entrance at one side so people can sit facing east," said one trustee. The other trustee disagreed. "A flat roof and a side entrance looks like a union hall, not a synagogue. No, it should have a pitched roof with windows that come to an arch at the top, and a centre entrance." "Then it'll look just like the United Church," argued the first. Dreyfus again found himself in the middle. "Why not a flat roof and windows with arches, or a pitched roof with straight windows." "And what about the entrance," challenged my father, "where would you put that, in Sudbury?" Dreyfus thought a moment. "Why don't we hire an architect and settle it that way?" For once Crandel and my father saw as one. An architect was simply out of the question. The only architect in town was a Scotsman. What would he know about designing a synagogue? "There are Jewish architects in Toronto then . . ." Dreyfus said gingerly. The other two were against that idea as well. Crandel said flatly, "Delicatessen we can afford to import from Toronto. Architects we can't." And that was that.

Finally, the committee hired a draftsman to try to interpret the opposing concepts. Though his talent and imagination were minimal—he could draw a straight line with the assistance of a ruler and little more—the draftsman managed somehow to reduce the trustees' ideas to several exterior designs and interior floor plans. Again the controversy was submitted to a general meeting, and the nod went to a pitched roof with flat windows, and a centre entrance. The walls would be of red brick and the only exterior adornment would be a reproduction over the main doors of the tablets bearing the Ten Commandments.

Inexpensive, functional, and not too Gentile in appearance. The little renaissance bird, lying stricken in the middle of the vacant lot on Bruce Street, now gave a final gasp for breath and expired.

In both of these situations, there had not been a true consensus. Rather, there was a winner and a loser. At least, that's how Crandel and my father viewed matters. Dreyfus looked into the mirror as he shaved himself in the mornings and saw an increasingly unhappy middle-man, a man who could not remain non-aligned much longer. Between Crandel and my father the air was becoming too thick to breathe in, even for a man of Dreyfus' modest respiratory requirements.

"Why do I need this aggravation?" he would ask of his wife in the privacy of their kitchen. Watching her husband push aside a supper only half-eaten, observing how he stared wearily down at a glass of tea only half-drunk, his wife would respond in a word, "Resign." But Dreyfus could not resign, could not admit defeat, could not let these fleeting moments of history, these compelling events in the affairs of men, pass him by. His eye was on that shining day when the key would be turned and the front doors would be open for the first time to admit the congregation, and it would be said of him and his two fellow trustees: "They did it, by God they really did it!" There would be a price to pay, something more profound and costly than unfinished meals and glasses of tea turned cold. He knew that eventually circumstances would force him to take a side and in doing so he knew he would automatically gain a fearful enemy. Being a man with a conscience, Dreyfus asked himself over and over again: is this goal of mine worth such a price? And each time the answer came back: yes!

The agonies over the location and design of the synagogue were followed by other agonies in various dimensions. The cumulative effect of these confrontations between Crandel and my father changed the whole nature of the building committee. It now operated as a three-man parliament with Crandel and my father alternating roles as the party in power and the official opposition, and Dreyfus sitting uneasily in the speaker's chair. If Crandel said light, my father said dark. If my father said straight, Crandel said curved. Votes of non-confidence took place almost every time a shovelful of earth was about to be dug or a nail was about to be hammered into place. The unfortunate contractor, a local man who had never before been engaged to build a synagogue, stood by with shovel and hammer, eyes turned heavenward, wondering: why me?

Meanwhile the congregation's treasury had to be filled to meet mounting expenses. Two years had passed since the committee's appointment and thus far only the concrete foundation had been completed. Borrowing from their Christian counterparts, the women of the congregation became involved in the business of fund-raising. They ran teas and bake sales, sold rummage, staged fashion shows, operated raffles, knitted, sewed, quilted. Like internal revenue agents they swooped down—entirely unexpected—upon their husbands' poker games, skimming the cream off winners' pots and appropriating the proceeds for the synagogue. Following a rash of such "income tax raids," the husbands chose to tax themselves voluntarily, on the theory that it was better to give up ten percent of the pot on your own than to have your wife breathing over your shoulder when you were waiting to fill an inside straight.

The year 1944 became The Year Of The Ticket. Every-time a non-Jew turned around, he found a Jew standing behind him waiting to sell a ticket.

Though these efforts yielded significant financial returns, the project depended principally upon pledges of donation by the congregants. When it came to extracting donations, the fund-raisers displayed a mastery of the fine art of gentle brutality. Everyone knew everyone else's business—or thought he did. Thus, if a congregant appeared to pledge to the building fund less than what he was generally thought to be capable of contributing, he would arrive at his store one morning to find a two-man delegation waiting for him. The discussion then flowed like this:

HOST: So, they put you up to this, eh?

DELEGATION: They? Who's they? Nobody put us up to any-
              thing. We just want to have a little talk with
              you.

HOST: Save your breath. I'm very tight for money
              now. Maybe after the Christmas season. . .

DELEGATION: We happen to know you sold more winter
              coats this fall than you did in all the years
              you've been in business.

HOST: Who the hell said so?

DELEGATION: The manufacturers. Don't forget, we buy
              from them, too. They tell us enough—

HOST: They didn't tell you, did they, that I had to
              unload their lousy coats at half-price?

DELEGATION: You never ran an honest half-price sale in
              your life, you bullshitter, and you know it.
              Besides, everybody in this town knows you got
              so much cash hidden away in the bank that the
              manager is ready to ask you for a loan. Come
              on now, you can do better . . .

It was no use trying to wriggle and squirm, the vice was too tight. Out came the recalcitrant's chequebook and pen.

"Thank you, you're a real mensch," the delegation would say as it took leave. "Call us, maybe we'll play a little gin rummy tonight. But don't forget to bring money."

When all other pledges had been gathered, Crandel then announced his own pledge. It turned out to be the most generous of all, even larger than Der Reicher's. Indeed, it almost matched the combined pledges of the rest of the congregation. News of Crandel's munificence was greeted with general rejoicing. In the early spring of 1945 walls began to rise from the concrete foundation. After three years of work and worry, the end was at last in sight.

But the wrangling and tension within the building committee was far from ended. With each course of brick, each stud, each joist, each floorboard, some new crisis arose, Crandel insisting upon one thing, my father insisting upon the exact opposite and Dreyfus caught in the awful no-man's-land between the hostile armies watching the shells burst like starfire overhead. "Resign," his wife pleaded continually. "No, I must see it through," he insisted.

All during the preceding three years, I had managed to remain uninvolved. The building of the synagogue was adult territory and I was content to sit on the sidelines smirking cynically now and then when communal bickering rose to a noisy level. I reacted coolly whenever my father came home from a building committee meeting ablaze with fury because of some decision arbitrarily made by Crandel, or some vacillation on Dreyfus' part. "This is the way the damn fools do these things," I told myself. "Let them have their little power games." I had more important business in those days:

passing a test for a driver's licence, and exploring fresh horizons with young schiksas—horizons barely dreamed of in the old pre-mobile days and nights. There were carefree Saturdays and Sundays sitting with friends on the porch of the Boat Club, talking introspectively about our love lives. There loomed also the horrors of the final year of high school, that long last feast of facts and figures to be crammed into us for ten unrelieved months until we were totally constipated with knowledge. And after that? Who could be sure? If one survived the forced-feedings of Grade Thirteen there might be college and—more importantly—freedom in some big city in the east, probably Toronto. Der Reicher's words "not for us but for our children" were meaningful only to parents. As far as I and my few Jewish contemporaries were concerned, our elders might just as well have been erecting a dance hall.

Then, without warning, an event occurred that changed all of this and drew me into the synagogue affair as meat is drawn into a grinder.

October, 1945. The first rafters were being fitted into place, their inverted "V" shapes pointing skyward, giving the red brick building all at once a sense of height, even of loftiness. In the centuries-old record of religious architecture, this structure would never leave its mark, nor would pilgrims, a thousand years after, journey to this ground from far corners of the earth to inspect its ruins. Yet now, for the first time, our mothers and fathers—even those who had been most critical of location and design—talked of the day when the last drop of paint would be dry and the congregation would enjoy the novel experience of entering a house where they were landlord. There was excitement in the air. Despite all the tensions between Crandel and my father, and the grinding effect these had on Dreyfus, the project had gone forward—oftentimes limping—but always forward.

A special meeting of the congregation was held to hear the elaborate plans for consecration ceremonies, and view preliminary sketches of the interior details.

Then Crandel rose to speak. His face—old but handsome, with its full well-trimmed moustache—gave him the appearance of a retired field marshal in some turn-of-the-century Balkan kingdom. He spoke slowly and in a low voice, but being Crandel he commanded absolute attention.

"My friends, before long we will have to order a plaque over the main entrance to our synagogue. It should have the date of the opening, and I think we can now safely say that date will be 1946 . . ."

Nods of agreement, smiles of satisfaction, little utterances of pleasure (". . . thank God . . . at last . . . I didn't think we'd live to see the day . . ."). Crandel raised his arms, motioning the members to be silent again; then he continued, his voice so low that older people in the audience were obliged to lean forward in their chairs to hear better, and some had to cup their hands behind their ears to catch his words.

"The time has come to give our synagogue a name, and I think you will agree that this is a matter of considerable importance since the name must be carefully chosen . . ."

My father, who hadn't known that this would be on the agenda, looked across the room at Dreyfus whose chair was close to Crandel's. The suspicious frown on my father's face asked, "What's Crandel up to?" But Dreyfus pretended not to read the frown, and dropped his eyes to his hands which lay folded across his stomach. With the fingers of his right hand he played with a black and gold Masonic ring on his left hand, twisting it round and round nervously.

Perhaps for dramatic effect, perhaps because he too was

nervous, Crandel paused for a few seconds to study his audience. There were faces there he had known for many years, faces that were open and trusting, faces that were respectful and admiring. For was it not true that he was old and wise and the most generous of all in his devotion to the project and the giving of money? Was he not—in a way—Moses come to lead them out of the Foresters Hall and into their very own place of worship? They hung now in a state of suspense, waiting for whatever he might say to them. He began again.

"I would like to ask . . . I would like to *suggest* . . . that the synagogue should be named . . after my father . . ."

Crandel paused again, giving this last sentence time to sink in. Then he resumed, "As you know, it has been a cherished dream of mine for a long time to be able to honour my father's memory in this way. So now, I am asking you to give me that opportunity . . ."

Sensing that he had said enough in support of his cause, the old man removed his eyeglasses, placed them carefully in their case, and lowered himself laboriously into his chair. In an instant a dozen men sprang to their feet demanding to be heard. What followed was chaos. Everyone, it seemed, cherished the dream of honouring his own father's memory in that very same way. "After all," said the town's humblest Jew, "each of us gave the most he could according to his means. Why shouldn't all of us be given the privilege of having the synagogue named after our fathers? It's only fair . . ."

"Come come now," the president said, "be reasonable, my friends. We can't have a name that's a block long."

"Then let's have a lottery and the winner gets to choose the name," someone called out.

"But that's gambling, and you don't gamble over a name for a holy place," someone else protested.

Even Der Reicher, who took pride in remaining aloof from most synagogue controversies, dived into the troubled waters, insisting that his father's name appear over the entrance to the synagogue, a demand the congregation could not afford to take lightly since his pledge was almost as large as Crandel's. If he, like Crandel, were in any way offended and alienated, he might withdraw his financial support and such a move could spell disaster for the project.

Throughout the din, Crandel sat impassive, like a father patiently waiting for his obstreperous offspring to exhaust their tempers, confident that when all the hubub was over and done with they would comprehend the reasonableness of his request. But the din did not subside. It grew until all decorum disappeared. Vigorously the president pounded his gavel sending sharp cracks of rifle fire across the room, but to no avail. Members rose one after another without bothering to be recognized by the chair, shouting and cross-talking, issuing threats, delivering ultimatums, all in the name of honouring their fathers' memories. Crandel, holy man that he was, had led his tiny flock writhing and screaming into a black pit.

Realizing that the congregants were in no mood to listen to prayer or Talmudic wisdom, the rabbi sat by, shaking his head sadly. Would God, he wondered, choose this unfortunate hour to return from His long vacation? And if He did, would He—upon surveying the scene of bedlam and acrimony—order the heavenly Department of Public Works to start the Second Flood?

Only when Crandel finally stood again and raised his hands in a plea for silence was order restored.

"My friends," Crandel said, "I didn't think my simple request could cause such trouble. Please, I beg of you, be calm; try to understand how important the matter of the name is to me and to my family. May I remind you that to-morrow the building committee must meet with our bank manager, Mr. Leamington, to extend our loan so we can finish the building. As you know, my friends, I am a co-signer on our note to the bank and I have to make up my mind whether or not to continue to be responsible on that note. Therefore, I must know the general decision about the name as soon as possible——"

Before Crandel could go on, Der Reicher stood up, this time without his hands in his pockets, and, pointing a finger angrily at Crandel, shouted, "Just a minute. If you take your name off that note, I take mine off! I'm not going to stick my neck out alone."

"But, but, you can't do that!" Dreyfus stammered. "We won't be able to pay the contractors and the suppliers. They'll slap liens against us. There'll be court cases, scandals." Dreyfus looked over to my father, "Say something, for Godsake!"

Everyone in the room now turned to my father. He sat rigid, his face the colour of putty. Without rising from his chair, he looked directly at Crandel. Like long sharp icicles the words came out: "If they name the synagogue after his father, it will be over my dead body!"

Gasps of horror went up all around the meeting hall. Dreyfus rose, shook a fist angrily at my father, but was unable to utter a word, so overcome by revulsion was he. Moving to where Crandel was seated, he took the old man's hand and whispered in his ear. Whatever Dreyfus said was unimportant; it was the gesture that was significant. From that moment on, the Crandel-Dreyfus alliance was a fact.

I, too, was horrified by my father's conduct. It seemed to me that he had blackened himself at a crucial moment when some grand peace effort was so desperately needed. I had wanted him to do the noble thing, to yield to old Crandel, or to propose some brilliant compromise. Instead, he had summoned up all the bile that was in him, and had spilled it there on the floor of that meeting hall, and I was disappointed and ashamed.

I left my chair, which was next to his, and stalked out of the hall without saying a word to him, or looking back to see what his reaction was.

We avoided each other, my father and I, after he returned home from the meeting. The following morning we exchanged no conversation. "I'm going to the bank," my father said curtly. "Look after the store."

An hour later he was back, pressing a handkerchief to his cheek just under his left eye. I started to ask, "What the hell happened——" but he broke in.

"You see, you see what your hero did," he said, his voice trembling with fury. He removed the handkerchief to reveal a large red blotch.

"Where did it happen?"

"At the bank. He threatened to take back his note and his pledge——"

"And what did you say?"

"Never mind what I said. Till the day he dies he'll remember what I said."

"Let me get you a cold compress or something."

I started toward the washroom to fetch a wet towel.

"No!" he shouted, "I don't need your help. You walked out on me once. Now leave me alone. I don't need anybody's help."

There were charges and countercharges of assault and eventually Crandel and my father found themselves standing like two errant schoolboys in front of Magistrate McKewen. "You should be ashamed of yourselves," the old red-nosed Magistrate scolded, his tongue and throat still raw from the previous night's bottle of cheap rye. "Go home, the two of you, and don't let me see either of you in my court again. Case dismissed."

But that was not the end of it for Crandel, or for my father, or for me.

For many months afterward, my father languished in a state of bitterness, convinced that he had been betrayed by the congregation. The incident at the bank had resulted not in rebuke for Crandel, as my father had expected, but in an agreement to name the synagogue after Crandel's father. The project was solvent again and progressed without further interruption. Face-to-face meetings of the building committee were out of the question, of course. Through intermediaries Crandel-Dreyfus on one side, and my father on the other, communicated frequent messages of dispute ("the curtains should be navy blue, not maroon") and rare messages of agreement ("O.K. to pay plumber's bill").

The lines of communication between my father and me, meanwhile, barely stayed open.

It was the eve of Rosh Hashonah, a warm Indian Summer evening in 1946, and the first High Holy Days services ever to be held in the synagogue had just begun. The air was filled with a heady mixture of smells—perfume, mothballs, aftershave lotion, burning candlewax, old musty prayerbooks, damp plaster, fresh paint. Flanked by his three sons, the rabbi chanted in a deep baritone voice that seemed to have taken on a fresh full-throated quality in keeping with these new surroundings. Women sat, heads erect in bright new autumn millinery. Men inspected the well-cut lapels of their new suits and made certain to show the proper amount of white cuff at the sleeves. Kids tugged at tight shirt collars and showed off new shoes to each other, comparing shines which—in less than 24 hours—would disappear forever. The atmosphere was alive with festivity.

When the time for the reading from the Torah arrived, the rabbi leaned across his lectern and whispered something into the ear of the president of the congregation who sat next to him on the dais. The two men nodded.

"I should like to call to the reading of the blessings . . . Mr. Crandel," the rabbi's voice boomed.

Crandel stood up from his seat in the front pew. He smiled faintly at his wife, a small regal woman who resembled Queen Victoria. She smiled back at him, and nodded, as if encouraging him to go on. Slowly the old man advanced to the dais and mounted the steps. He shook the rabbi's hand, and the president's hand. Waving away an open prayerbook offered by the rabbi, Crandel turned and looked directly down at my father. He began to speak. "I want to say something . . ." His voice choked, and he attempted to speak again. "I want to say . . ." But the words were trapped deep within his throat, or locked still deeper within his tired old heart, words that were incapable of freeing themselves and taking to the still air. Unable to say anything, Crandel held out his arms in the direction of my father.

During a long moment in which everyone and everything within that sanctuary seemed frozen, Crandel's outstretched hands hovered in the air, palms turned upward, inviting, imploring, begging to be accepted. My father turned away. "I can't . . . I won't . . . No . . ." Voices everywhere around him spoke to him urgently, those nearby whispering, others further away calling out, "Go . . . take his hand . . . be a mensch . . . you can't just let him stand there . . . go! . . ." Arms reached out from all sides, tugging his arms, pressing him to move from where he sat stubbornly rooted. " Go now . . . now . . ."

Mumbling to no one in particular, "Dammit, dammit to hell!" my father left his seat. He climbed the three steps of the dais, taking them one at a time slowly and deliberately as if to put off as long as possible the awful moment when his hand would meet Crandel's. Impulsively, Crandel lurched forward and threw his heavy arms around my father's shoulders, drawing the younger man toward him with such force that both men nearly toppled over. My father made no move to resist Crandel's encirclement, and his arms merely hung locked at his sides. Neither man uttered a word.

Two jagged chunks of granite, dislodged from separate mountain peaks, had landed against each other in the valley below. They could roll no further and would have to share that ground then and forever.

Eyes are all I remember about the next minute or two. Dreyfus removed his spectacles and pressed the palms of his hands to his eyes to rub away the tears. Old Crandel dabbed at his eyes with a handkerchief as he turned his back to the congregation and prepared to say the blessings. My father dabbed at his eyes with a handkerchief as he stepped from the dais and walked briskly up the aisle between the pews with me trailing behind him. On either side of the aisle eyes were upon us—most of them moist and red-rimmed.

I expected my father to take a seat at the rear of the sanctuary where there was always a vacant pew, and where he might regain his composure. Instead he hurried through the exit not bothering to close the door behind him, and started to march down Bruce Street toward Queen, his steps coming down hard on the sidewalk, his body bent forward against a non-existent wind. It was the march of a man burning with emotions—embarrassment, shame, anger. I was obliged to take extra-long strides just to remain two or three paces behind him. Not until he came to the first corner, at Bruce and Albert, did he halt, and as he waited for passing traffic before continuing, I caught up. Without looking at me, but staring straight ahead, he said hoarsely, "You see, you damn fool; you thought temples are built by saints, didn't you? Well now you know, it's not saints that accomplish anything in this lousy world, it's sonsofbitches."

"I never said you were a son of a bitch."

"And if I was, so what? It shouldn't have made one goddam bit of difference to you. I was no worse than the rest of them. You had no right to look down on me, to desert me, to betray me."

I took a very deep breath. "I'm sorry," I said.

Refusing still to look at me as I stood there on the streetcorner beside him, he went on, the rage and bitterness of past months leaking through his words, his voice barely under control. "Sons are meant to stand by their fathers, not to kick them in the face when they are down. The Bible says even if your father disgraces you, you cover him with a blanket and hide your eyes; you don't call in the whole world and shout 'look what a bastard my father is!' "

I wanted to say, "But I can't stand by *anybody* that much. It's just not in me." All I said, however, was, "I'm sorry. What more can I say?"

"That's alright," he responded, voice still hoarse and unsteady. "Someday you'll have your chance to get even with me. When you're a man and I'm dead you can piss on my grave all you want."

He resumed his march down Bruce Street toward Queen Street without looking to see if I was following or not. But I knew that I had been forgiven.

The Messiah
of Second-Hand Goods

Throughout his life my father was a missionary who combed the streets offering shelter and salvation to all sorts of world-weary goods—odd remnants of cloth, bent nails, used lumber, rusty tools. Over the years, the basement beneath his store became a hostel for a vast collection of castaway property. Each and every item in that collection he hoarded against the improbable day when it might come in handy.

During one of my last visits with him, my father confessed to me, in anguish, that the local fire department inspector had declared the place a hazard. Worse still, my father's insurance agent heartily endorsed the inspector's verdict.

"The bastards are in cahoots," he said bitterly.

"You mean, it's a conspiracy?" I asked, pretending to be horrified. "You think they really want all that stuff for themselves?"

"Why not? I bet between the two of them they haven't got a pot to piss in."

"They'll find one in your basement, that's for sure."

"If you're such a smart guy," my father said, sliding the phone book across his desk at me, "then call the sonsofbitches and tell 'em they can't force me to clear it all out."

"I can't do that," I protested. "At least, not until I've had a chance to study your insurance policy and the local fire regulations."

"I thought you're a lawyer—"

"I am."

"Then how come you don't know these things?"

"I was absent from law school the day they took 'Junk Collections.' Just give me fifteen minutes please and I'll have some answers for you."

A half-hour later I was ready with my report. My father glanced impatiently at his watch. "What took so long, Lawyer? You're an hour late already."

"I read your policy and talked with the inspector—"

"And?"

"And they're right. It is a hazard. You'll have to clear out the basement, that's all there is to it."

"For this I needed a lawyer in the family? I could've got better advice from a doctor."

I could feel my face reddening and suddenly my shirt-collar felt two sizes too small for my neck. "Let's not get into that lawyer-versus-doctor routine again. I'm thirty-seven years old and there's no way I'm going to medical school at this point in my life. It's about time you got used to the idea."

"With those hands," my father said, shaking his head sadly, "you would've made a brilliant surgeon."

"Don't change the subject. I'm a lawyer and I tell you the City is going to lay a charge against you under one of the bylaws. What's more, your insurance may be cancelled."

"I just don't understand it. Why all of a sudden now, after I've been in this place nearly thirty years?"

"Because last week—in case you didn't know it—was Fire

Prevention Week."

"Fire Prevention Week?" My father was unimpressed. "That's for little kids, to teach them they shouldn't play with matches. What the hell has Fire Prevention Week got to do with me?"

"They're afraid you'll burn down the entire town. Like Mrs. O'Leary's cow."

"Mrs. O'Leary's cow took place in Chicago. This is Sault Ste. Marie."

"They claim you've got enough flammable material in the cellar to burn down Chicago too."

He refused to be convinced of the potential danger. Besides, he pointed out, he'd spent a lifetime accumulating the collection. "My God," he pleaded, "there's a goldmine down there, now."

To prove it, he conducted me on a tour of that dank subterranean space, and we squeezed ourselves along a narrow aisle that parted mountains of cardboard cartons, wooden boxes, and old steamer trunks. Spread out around me was a museum stuffed full of unremarkable objects, most of which should have been condemned to the rubbish heap years ago. I let out a low whistle of astonishment. "You sure don't believe in travelling light in this world," I commented.

He ignored me and gave his attention instead to a pile of round iron bars that lay on the floor near his feet, counting and re-counting them. "That's funny," he said, "there's only eleven and I could swear I had an even dozen."

"What're you planning to do with them?" I asked, picking up one of the bars.

"I'm thinking of opening a jail, schmeckle," he answered, taking the bar from me and replacing it carefully on the pile.

I raised the lid on a large carton of men's rubber footwear. "What are you saving these for?"

"World War Three. They'll be worth a fortune. First thing that's short in a war is rubbers."

"How come they didn't sell in World War Two?"

"The sizes were too large."

"What makes you think they'll go over big in the next war?"

"People's feet are getting longer; it's a fact."

Crammed in a dark corner was an uncomfortable quartet of derelict female mannequins, their wigless heads almost touching the low joists overhead, their nude featureless bodies frozen into stiff unnatural poses. "And when do you expect to use *them* again?" I asked.

"Their time will come," he replied confidently.

"Do you really think women will ever look like that again? They haven't even got any nipples on their breasts."

"Nipples I can always buy in a drug store."

"Look," I said, "let's be serious."

"I am serious. You're the one who's treating this whole thing like a joke."

I tried to sound sympathetic. "I'm sure all this stuff means a great deal to you, and maybe some of it should be kept."

"Some of it!" he exploded. "You're all alike—you, the fire inspector, my wonderful insurance agent. Easy come, easy go; that's all you people know."

"Take it easy."

"Take it easy my ass! I'm not moving one stick, one nail, one piece of thread out of this basement. I'll set fire to it myself first."

After years of training, I had learned to walk away from the blowtorch of his temper. "You're crazy," I said quietly. And I turned and made my way through the narrow canyon that led out of the basement. I left him standing behind me in the aisle, in the company of the four hairless mannequins, calling after me, "I'm not crazy, the whole world's crazy; I'm the only one with any brains!"

All during the return flight from the Soo to Toronto I could think of nothing else but the man bellowing back there in that basement. How did he become the Messiah of Second-hand Goods? How does anyone become a Messiah? Is it all in the way one is conceived?

My father was conceived on the rear platform of a horse-drawn cart, between bundles of clothing and an assortment of pots and pans, one black winter night while his parents were in full flight from a band of drunken Cossacks. It was the time of the annual pogrom, when Jews in that part of Russia were once again "in season" and were picked off in bunches, the way ripe strawberries are ravaged by hungry bears.

These were hours of frantic activity. Russian swords were swung and guns were fired. Jewish household goods were flung into wagons at midnight. Flames crackled in barns. Horses were whipped and cursed at to go faster along the back-country roads. In the midst of a frantic dash for the safety of the forests, my paternal grandfather—ever mindful of the uncertainties of tomorrow—entrusted his horse's reins to Fate, and there—in the back of their clattering cart—he and his wife pitched and rolled together, encouraged by sudden passion, and assisted by the rocky contour of the road.

Thus did my father come into being.

How do I know this?

I don't. There's nothing in the family records to bear witness—who would record such an act anyway? Certainly my father—gifted as he was with hindsight—remembered noth-

ing of the precise circumstances, and if he did, he saw fit to
disclose nothing. No matter. I have a photograph of my
father's parents that tells all. There they stand, in their
seventies, looking more like an old pair of boots than man
and wife. There is snow on the ground and their faces are
fierce and frostbitten. "Get on with it," they seem to be
saying, "take the damn picture before we freeze to death
here!" That they are being preserved on film for posterity
is of little importance to them at this moment. Hurry up,
get on with it. For today it's the winter that oppresses. And
tomorrow it'll be the Russians again. And the day after—
who knows?

Who knows?

There was another possible explanation for my father's
nature: the devils in his life. Of them my father spoke frequently. Descendants of the demons that inhabited his
boyhood home in Russia, these mid-twentieth century devils
were much more innovative and proficient than their European predecessors when it came to fouling things up. Apply-
ing contemporary techniques to ancient evils, they hovered
over the stock market in his later years, casting sinister
lights and shadows over his investments so that each speculation rose hopefully, plunged sharply, then levelled off
many points below his aspirations. Sardonic memos in his
diary summed up each day's luckless ventures: "Sold today
500 shares Consolidated Crap, bought 300 shares International Garbage." The same devils concocted overnight
changes in the length of women's dresses so that yesterday's
saleable garments became transformed into today's give-
away rags. Like vampires, certain of the devils bled his cash
register to pay income taxes, sales taxes, property taxes, and
a hundred other levies imposed by other devils. Like masters
of psychological warfare, they caused his love affairs to run

aground on reefs of suspicion and jealousy. Like experts of chemical warfare, they poisoned old friendships and turned them sour.

Nature conspired against him. People could no longer be trusted. At this stage of his existence he believed in, and loved, only those things he could truly possess: land, buildings, chattels of every description. He loved things that could be spoken to and relied upon not to talk back, touched and relied upon not to bite; things that could be polished and were guaranteed to remain brilliant; that could be stored without aging and rotting; that could be nailed down, locked up, buried away from the sun in chests and closets without ever clamouring for freedom.

He loved equipment: tools, shovels, rakes, polishing cloths, paint brushes. He loved his sixteen-foot runabout with the silver-green outboard motor, and his fishing rods lined up absolutely parallel with each other.

He loved everything in its place. He loved horizontals and verticals, ninety-degree angles and perfect circles.

Whenever I brought my wife and children from Toronto to visit, he would greet us with wide-eyed enthusiasm, like a hermit happy to be discovered at last in his cave. But within twenty-four hours the smells of furniture wax and mothballs came between us and it was apparent that we were intruders in his world of order and timeliness. On the final day of our visit, he would begin to restore everything in the cave to its exact pre-arrival position, even before our bags were packed.

Whenever it came time to say goodbye to my father, we didn't depart—we checked out.

Six months after the local fire inspector ordered him to

jettison all that excess cargo in the hold, my father learned from a chest specialist that he might also have to dispose of one of his lungs.

"I can never understand all that Latin baloney. What did the doctor call it again?" my father asked.

"He called it a slight irregularity, a minor tissue change." I tried to adopt the same casual manner displayed that morning by the doctor, tried to sound like a mechanic easing the mind of a Sunday driver whose engine had overheated. "On the X ray it just shows as a tiny white spot."

"I didn't ask you to describe it in English. English I could understand. What did he call it in Latin?"

"I don't remember—"

"I heard it before, once. Carson-something."

"I tell you I don't remember—"

He snapped his fingers. "I remember. Carcinoma, that was it. What's it mean, exactly?"

"How should I know?"

"You're a lawyer aren't you? How come you don't know Latin?"

"I was away the day they took 'Carcinoma.'"

"You must have been away a lot of days," he said, looking at me out of the corners of his eyes, shrewdly; he knew I was lying.

"Carcinoma happens to be a medical, not a legal, term."

He sighed. "You would know what it means if you had gone to medical school like I wanted."

"Okay, I'll make a deal with you," I said, inspired. "You submit to a biopsy, like the doctor recommended, and I'll apply for admission to any medical school you say. Is it a deal?"

"Are you crazy, or are you just out of your mind?" he retorted. "You really think I'm going to let those butchers play around with my insides?"

"I thought you worshipped doctors. Now all of a sudden they don't know what they're doing? You are incredible!"

"What's so incredible? You take Bill Lundy, the plumber. Looked like a million dollars. Went to the hospital for a hernia and never came out. Take for instance Tom Mc-Latchey. Remember him? Strong like a bull; used to carry a tool box that weighed a ton. They found something in his stomach and he died right there on the operating table. And what about Milt Hershbaum, the traveller, wasn't he the picture of health? So what do you think happened to him? He went to some fancy clinic in Boston for a checkup—so help me God, a lousy checkup!—and they killed him and shipped his body home in a box."

"Alright, so Lundy and McLatchey and Milt whats-his-name had tough luck. What does that prove? Thousands upon thousands of people come out of hospitals cured. The exceptions are not the rule."

"It's always my luck to be an exception. Besides, I could tell from the way the doctor acted that I'm a goner. You and the doctor suppose maybe that I'm a yokel from Shtipo-vitz, don't you? Well I happen to have a damn good idea what Carcinoma means. It's a fifty-dollar word for cancer."

"Goddamit!" I yelled, furious. "Here I've been making an honest effort to keep the truth from you; the least you could have done was to make an honest effort to keep it from me. You're one helluva lousy sport!"

"I'm sorry. I never had cancer before. Nobody ever told me it's a game and I'm supposed to be a good sport."

"Listen to me," I said, calming down. "You're not a goner. The doctor says it's at an early stage and if you'd undergo this biopsy—"

"Ach, what do doctors know? Look what they did to poor

Sarah Blackstein. Cut her up and sent her back to Sam in pieces. A real mess. Know what he told me confidentially? He says it's like sleeping with a jigsaw puzzle."

"But a biopsy is a fairly simple procedure."

"Alright alright, I'll have the biopsy. Just leave me alone already."

"You will? When?"

"Soon."

"When?"

"When I'm ready."

"When will that be?"

"When I've looked after all my things. First things first."

"What things?"

"Everything. I want to check over everything, organize all my things, see they're stored properly."

"You can do all that when you get out of the hospital."

"And suppose I don't get out of the hospital? Don't forget what happened to Benny Koffman. I bet he wasn't a day over fifty when—"

"Forget Benny Koffman, will you. There's no need for that now. Time is of the essence."

"Like I said before, first things first. I have to do what I have to do. That's my way."

"I'll stay here for a few days and look after your precious things."

"Like hell you will. The minute I'm out cold on the operating table you'll hire a couple of husky Talyainer and a truck and haul the whole kit and caboodle out of here. Just like you wanted to do when that low-life from Fire Prevention Week thought he discovered a volcano in my building."

"That low-life did you a favour."

"It's the other way around," my father said, slyly. "I did him a favour. I had him bring his wife into the store—you should have seen her—like a stray cat searching for milk, that's how she looked. But when she walked out of the store she looked like the Queen of Sheba. After that, I could've planted an atomic bomb down there and they would've given me a gold medal!"

"In other words, all that crap is still in the basement?"

"Every bit of it," he exulted.

"Look," I said, raising my right hand, "I solemnly promise not to touch one stick, one nail, one piece of thread down there. I'll put it in writing if you don't trust me. I'll even swear an affidavit."

Seizing my arm firmly, but smiling patiently, he said, "You don't understand. If you want me to save my life, that's very nice of you. I appreciate it and I thank you very much. But you've got to let me save it my way."

I tore my arm away. "I know what you're up to," I said, "but you're not going to pin this on me—"

"Pin what? What're you talking about?"

"I'm wise to your little game. You want me to feel guilty about all this, don't you? Look at dear old Dad, everyone— standing there in that lousy basement gift-wrapping all those precious goodies for his little boy to inherit someday, and look at his little boy sitting in the meantime on his ass on the Riviera, sunning himself. I get the whole picture. It's the old Frederic Chopin routine again."

"Frederic who?"

"Chopin. In that movie *A Song to Remember?* He's supposed to be dying of t.b. but he insists on playing one last concert to raise money for Polish freedom. They even show him coughing blood all over the goddam keyboard. But good old Fred keeps right on playing to the very last drop, and at the end of the number—when he gets up from the piano —he makes a point of falling on his ass so the whole of

Poland will feel good and guilty. And that's exactly what you're doing now—leaving me a basement full of guilt!"

"I thought you said a minute ago you weren't going to let me pin my sickness on you."

"That's right, I'm not going to accept any guilt in this matter."

"Then what the hell are you worried about?"

"I'm worried that you're going to die and neither of us will really have understood each other. Yes, I suppose that's it. I simply cannot understand any man whose priorities in this world are so screwed up."

"And I can't understand any man who doesn't have the slightest idea of what it means to have things, to own things, to start with nothing and end with something, to buy, pay off mortgages, to say this is mine and some day it'll be my son's. You don't understand me, and I don't understand you. But that's alright with me. You don't have to understand me. Just live your life and remember me. I don't give a damn how; you can light a candle once a year, blow your car horn, turn on the furnace, any way you want is okay by me. To remember is necessary; to understand isn't."

Later that day the plane carrying me back to Toronto flew along the shoreline of the St. Mary's River before veering southeast toward Lake Huron. In the distance to my left I could just barely make out the intersection of Queen and Bruce Streets and—a little to the east of it—my father's building. At that very moment I knew that he was in the bedroom I had occupied the night before. I saw him smoothing the creases in the bedspread, puffing the pillow where my head had left an indentation, picking up bits of lint from the rug where I had stood, running a finger along the bureau where I'd spilled some talc. Each lamp was being repositioned to within a fraction of an inch of where it had

stood prior to my arrival. Each picture on the wall was re-
arranged dead level with the floor.

I had checked out of his house for the last time.

Within a year of the local fire inspector's report, my
father was dead of cancer. And these are what he left me: a
basement full of "things"; many puzzles (some of which I
have managed to solve and some of which I haven't); and
—every day, every night—car horns blowing, furnaces turning
on, and candles burning in my mind.